The World Wide Web Fe_____ng
Microsoft®
Internet Explorer 5
Illustrated Brief

Donald I. Barker
Chia-Ling H. Barker

ONE MAIN STREET, CAMBRIDGE, MA 02142

an *International Thomson Publishing company* I(T)P®

_____

Cambridge • Albany • Bonn • Boston • Cincinnati • London • Madrid • Melbourne • Mexico City
New York • Paris • San Francisco • Singapore • Tokyo • Toronto • Washington

The World Wide Web Featuring Microsoft® Internet Explorer 5 — Illustrated Brief

is published by Course Technology

Senior Product Manager:	Katie Schooling
Associate Product Manager:	Emily Heberlein
Contributing Author:	Sasha Vodnik
Development Editor:	Jeanne Herring
Production Editor:	Jennifer Hambly
Composition House:	GEX, Inc.
QA Manuscript Reviewer:	John Bosco
Text Designer:	Joseph Lee
Cover Designer:	Joseph Lee

© 1999 by Course Technology—I(T)P®

For more information contact:

Course Technology
One Main Street
Cambridge, MA 02142

ITP Europe
Berkshire House 168-173
High Holborn
London WCIV 7AA
England

Nelson ITP/Australia
102 Dodds Street
South Melbourne, 3205
Victoria, Australia

ITP Nelson Canada
1120 Birchmount Road
Scarborough, Ontario
Canada M1K 5G4

International Thomson Editores
Seneca 53
Colonia Polanco
11560 Mexico D.F. Mexico

ITP GmbH
Königswinterer Strasse 418
53227 Bonn
Germany

ITP Asia
60 Albert Street, #15-01
Albert Complex
Singapore 189969

ITP Japan
Hirakawacho Kyowa Building, 3F
2-2-1 Hirakawacho
Chiyoda-ku, Tokyo 102
Japan

Trademarks

Course Technology and the Open Book logo are registered trademarks of Course Technology.

Illustrated Projects and the Illustrated Series are trademarks of Course Technology.

I(T)P® The ITP logo is a registered trademark of International Thomson Publishing Inc.

Some of the product names and company names used in this book have been used for identification purposes only and may be trademarks or registered trademarks of their respective manufacturers and sellers.

Disclaimer

Course Technology reserves the right to revise this publication and make changes from time to time in its content without notice.

ISBN 0-7600-6054-1

Printed in the United States of America

2 3 4 5 6 7 8 9 BM 03 02 01 00

Enhance Any Illustrated Text With These Exciting Products!

Course CBT

Enhance your students' Office 2000 classroom learning experience with self-paced computer-based training on CD-ROM. Course CBT engages students with interactive multimedia and hands-on simulations that reinforce and complement the concepts and skills covered in the textbook. All the content is aligned with the MOUS (Microsoft Office User Specialist) program, making it a great preparation tool for the certification exams. Course CBT also includes extensive pre- and post-assessments that test students' mastery of skills. These pre- and post-assessments automatically generate a "custom learning path" through the course that highlights only the topics students need help with.

Course Assessment

How well do your students *really* know Microsoft Office? Course Assessment is a performance-based testing program that measures students' proficiency in Microsoft Office 2000. Previously known as SAM, Course Assessment is available for Office 2000 in either a live or simulated environment. You can use Course Assessment to place students into or out of courses, monitor their performance throughout a course, and help prepare them for the MOUS certification exams.

Create Your Ideal Course Package with CourseKits™

If one book doesn't offer all the coverage you need, create a course package that does. With Course Technology's CourseKits—our mix-and-match approach to selecting texts—you have the freedom to combine products from more than one series. When you choose any two or more Course Technology products for one course, we'll discount the price and package them together so your students can pick up one convenient bundle at the bookstore.

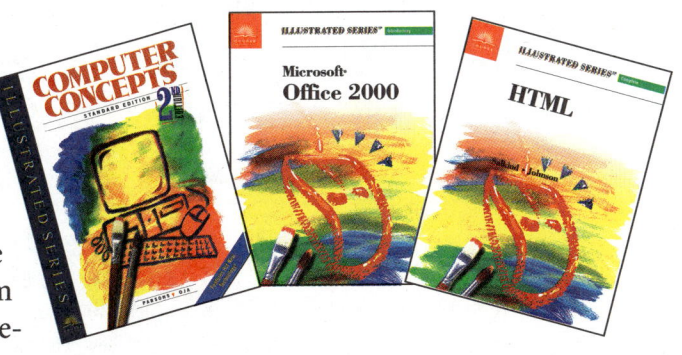

For more information about any of these offerings or other Course Technology products, contact your sales representative or visit our web site at:

www.course.com

Preface

Welcome to *The World Wide Web Featuring Microsoft Internet Explorer 5 — Illustrated Brief.* This highly visual book offers new users a hands-on introduction to the World Wide Web and Internet Explorer and also serves as an excellent reference for future use.

► Organization and Coverage

This text contains four units that cover the basic skills necessary for Web browsing. In these units students learn how to use Internet Explorer 5 to navigate, search, and explore the Web.

► About this Approach

What makes the Illustrated approach so effective at teaching software skills? It's quite simple. Each skill is presented on two facing pages, with the step-by-step instructions on the left page, and large screen illustrations on the right. Students can focus on a single skill without having to turn the page. This unique design makes information extremely accessible and easy to absorb, and provides a great reference for after the course is over. This hands-on approach also makes it ideal for both self-paced or instructor-led classes.

Each lesson, or "information display," contains the following elements:

Each 2-page spread focuses on a single skill or concept.

Concise text introduces the basic principles discussed in the lesson. Procedures are easier to learn when concepts fit into a framework.

Internet

Working with Menus and Toolbars

For many operations, Internet Explorer provides several ways to complete the same task, using either menus or the toolbar. Although the menus in Internet Explorer contain the available commands and options, the toolbars, shown in Figure A-6, offer a quicker and easier way to access frequently used commands. Table A-2 briefly describes the buttons on the Standard Buttons toolbar. ▬ You can use the Explorer window controls to browse for more information on the World Wide Web. Familiarize yourself with these options to learn how they can help you work more efficiently as you market the Nut Tree products online.

Steps

QuickTip
Click the list arrow on the right side of the Address text box to display the names of the pages you have visited recently and to display the list of your computer's drives. To revisit a Web page or to open another document from your computer, simply click its name on the list.

1. Click **View** on the menu bar, then click **Refresh**
   Because your home page hasn't changed, the document window loads and displays the same page, as shown in Figure A-7. Although the page appears the same in this instance, **refreshing**, or reloading, a Web page is an important capability that ensures that you see the most recent version of a Web page. Explorer saves pages that you visit in a file on your computer, called a **cache**, to reduce loading time. The content on the Web changes continually, however, and using Refresh guarantees that you view the most up-to-date information.

2. Click the **Refresh button** [ ] on the Standard toolbar
   If reloading takes more than a few seconds, the status indicator (the Explorer logo) changes repeatedly. When the status indicator stops switching between images, the page has been successfully reloaded.

3. Click [ ] once more, this time quickly clicking the **Stop button** [ ] on the toolbar before the home page finishes reloading
   If you act quickly enough, the home page appears without graphics or other page elements. The Stop button offers a convenient way to halt the lengthy loading process of a page laden with images and other large elements. You will use it often when accessing the Web over a slow Internet connection such as a modem.

4. Click [ ] once more to fully load the page

CLUES TO USE

The appearance of toolbars

Internet Explorer 5 takes a unique and useful approach to displaying the toolbars. You can display the sections in a stacked fashion or you can consolidate them into a single row, providing more room for viewing a Web page. By default, Explorer displays the Links and Address Bar toolbars in a single row. To view the Radio toolbar, click View on the Menu bar, point to Toolbars, then click Radio. The Radio toolbar shares the row with the Address and Links toolbars. To expand the toolbars,

you can drag the heavy border bar at the bottom of the toolbar down, to fully display one or both of the consolidated toolbars. To redisplay the areas in the consolidated layout, simply drag the heavy toolbar border up. In the consolidated display, the Address Bar, Links toolbar and Radio toolbar share a single row, giving some of them the appearance of a button, by default. You can drag the double-ruled borders between them to change the amount of each toolbar that is exposed.

► IE A-8 GETTING STARTED WITH THE WORLD WIDE WEB

Clues to Use boxes provide concise information that either expands on one component of the major lesson skill or describes an independent task that is in some way related to the major lesson skill.

Tips as well as trouble-shooting advice right where you need it—next to the step itself.

Clear step-by-step directions explain how to complete the specific task. Material to be clicked, selected, or typed appears in red. When students follow the numbered steps, they quickly learn how each procedure is performed and what the results will be.

Every lesson features large, full-color representations of what the students' screen should look like after completing the numbered steps.

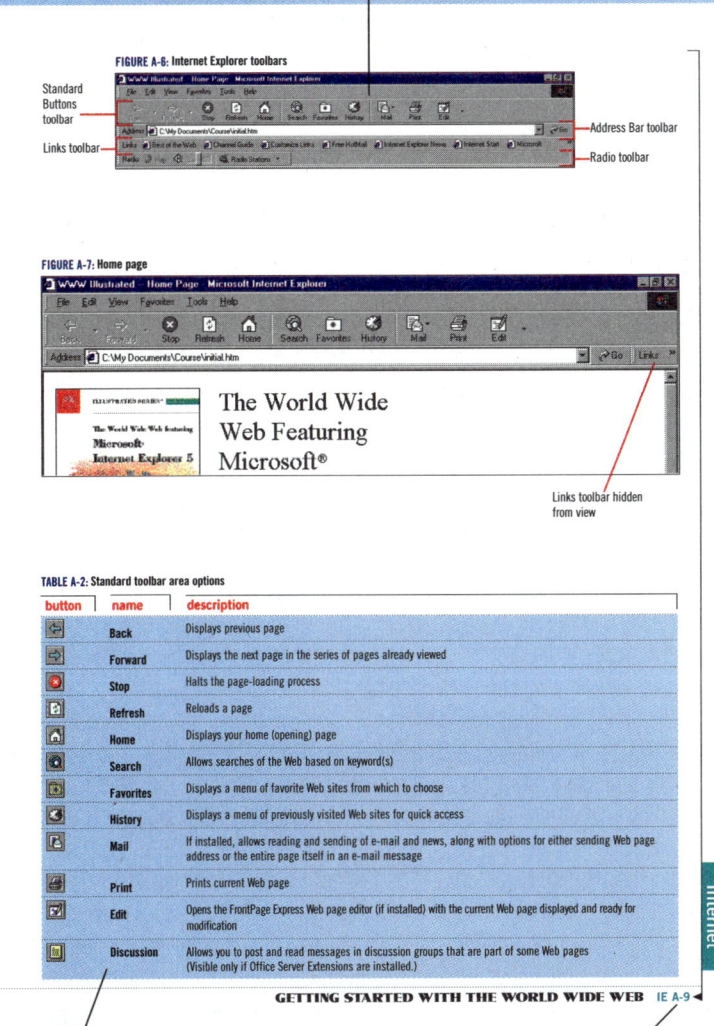

FIGURE A-6: Internet Explorer toolbars

Standard Buttons toolbar

Links toolbar

Address Bar toolbar

Radio toolbar

FIGURE A-7: Home page

The World Wide Web Featuring Microsoft®

Links toolbar hidden from view

TABLE A-2: Standard toolbar area options

button	name	description
	Back	Displays previous page
	Forward	Displays the next page in the series of pages already viewed
	Stop	Halts the page-loading process
	Refresh	Reloads a page
	Home	Displays your home (opening) page
	Search	Allows searches of the Web based on keyword(s)
	Favorites	Displays a menu of favorite Web sites from which to choose
	History	Displays a menu of previously visited Web sites for quick access
	Mail	If installed, allows reading and sending of e-mail and news, along with options for either sending Web page address or the entire page itself in an e-mail message
	Print	Prints current Web page
	Edit	Opens the FrontPage Express Web page editor (if installed) with the current Web page displayed and ready for modification
	Discussion	Allows you to post and read messages in discussion groups that are part of some Web pages (Visible only if Office Server Extensions are installed.)

Internet

GETTING STARTED WITH THE WORLD WIDE WEB   IE A-9

Quickly accessible summaries of key terms, toolbar buttons, or keyboard alternatives connected with the lesson material. Students can easily refer to this information when working on their own projects at a later time.

The page numbers are designed like a road map. A indicates the first unit and 9 indicates the page within the unit.

Other Features

The two-page lesson format featured in this book provides the new user with a powerful learning experience. Additionally, this book contains the following features:

▶ Real-World Skills
The skills used throughout the textbook are designed to be "real-world" in nature and representative of the kinds of activities that students encounter when working with Internet Explorer. With a real-world case, the process of solving problems will be more meaningful to students.

▶ End of Unit Material
Each unit concludes with a Concepts Review that tests students' understanding of what they learned in the unit. The Concepts Review is followed by a Skills Review, which provides students with additional hands-on practice of the skills they learned in the unit. The Skills Review is followed by Independent Challenges, which pose case problems for students to solve. The Visual Workshops allow students to learn by exploring and to develop critical thinking skills. Students are shown an existing Web page and asked to locate it on the Web.

▶ Student Online Companion
This text includes an innovative Student Online Companion that contains all the links necessary to complete the lessons and End of Unit Material in the book. These links are continually updated to insure that students access the most up-to-date information for the assignments.

Instructor's Resource Kit

The Instructor's Resource Kit is Course Technology's way of putting the resources and information needed to teach and learn effectively into your hands. With an integrated array of teaching and learning tools that offers you and your students a broad range of technology-based instructional options, we believe this kit represents the highest quality and most cutting edge resources available to instructors today. Many of these resources are available at www.course.com. The resources available with this book are:

Home Page   This book features its own home page, which is provided with the Project Files. See the inside front cover for more information on the Project Files. The Readme file accompanying the Project Files contains instructions for installation of the book's home page as the default home page on your browser.

Student Online Companion and Student Offline Companion Available at *www.course.com/ illustrated/ie5*, the innovative Online Companion enhances and augments the printed page by bringing students onto the Web for a dynamic and continually updated learning experience. The Student Online companion contains all of the links necessary to complete the lessons and End Of Unit Material.

Student Offline Companion   This companion allows students to work through all the lessons and most of the exercises in the book without Internet access. Instructions for the installation of the Offline Companion are in the ReadMe file that accompanies the Offline Companion files. Adopters of this text are granted the right to post the files on any standalone computer or network. The Offline Companion files are available on the Review Pack. Call your Customer Service Representative for more details.

Course Faculty Online Companion   You can browse this text's password-protected site to obtain everything needed to prepare for class. These periodically updated items include lesson plans, solutions, additional problems, and updates and revisions to the text. Contact your Customer Service Representative for the site address and password.

Online Instructor's Manual   Available at the Faculty Online Companion page. Quality assurance tested and includes:
- Solutions to all lessons and end-of-unit material
- Detailed lecture topics for each unit with teaching tips
- Extra Independent Challenges
- Project Files

Before You Begin   *The World Wide Web featuring Microsoft, Internet Explorer 5 - Illustrated Brief* is used in concert with the Student Online Companion or the Student Offline Companion. The student home page (initial.htm) and its accompanying file (cover.bmp) provide links to the Student Online Companion or Student Offline Companion; the lessons are written with the assumption that this student home page is the home page loaded on the students' browsers. The home page files can be found on the Review Pack in the \SETUP directory of the Project Files or downloaded from *www.course.com* with the Project Files.

A new feature of Microsoft, Internet Explorer 5 is the customizable toolbars. Using the new toolbars, resetting them to the default, and finding buttons or commands that are not visible on the toolbars are explained in Unit B. In all screen shots and steps, the authors have assumed that students are using the default toolbar settings.

To use Internet Explorer 5, you will need a 486/66 processor. A Pentium processor is recommended for Windows 95, Windows 98, or Windows NT 4.0, or use Digital PC AXP/150 MHz for Windows NT 4.0 for DEC Alpha.

The Operating System needed is Windows 95 or Windows 98 or Windows NT 4.0 (if you are running Windows NT 4.0, you must download Windows NT Service Pack 3 or higher).

The memory requirements are 16MB RAM for Windows 95 or Windows 98 and 32MB RAM for Windows NT 4.0. The disk space required to Run Internet Explorer: 27MB for browser-only, 55MB for typical installation, 78MB for full installation

Contents

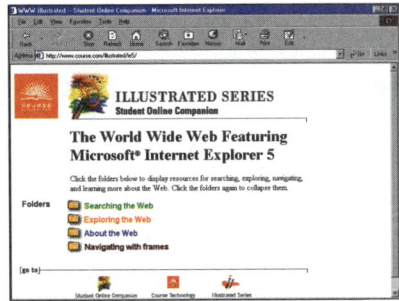

Contents

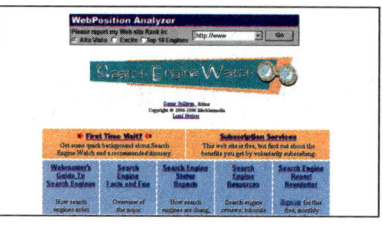

Getting
Started with the World Wide Web

▶ **Understand Microsoft Internet Explorer 5**
▶ **Start Internet Explorer**
▶ **Investigate the Internet Explorer window**
▶ **Work with menus and toolbars**
▶ **Move around a Web page**
▶ **Find text**
▶ **Get Help**
▶ **Print a Web page**
▶ **Exit Internet Explorer**

This unit introduces you to the World Wide Web and Microsoft Internet Explorer browsing software and add-ons. As you become familiar with Internet Explorer, you will discover it provides many useful tools for accessing the World Wide Web. You have just been hired as assistant to the marketing manager for The Nut Tree Company, a company that sells confectionaries and assorted nuts in attractive custom gift packaging. You will use Microsoft Internet Explorer software to investigate and establish a presence on the World Wide Web to help your company expand its business. You will begin by exploring the World Wide Web and the Internet Explorer environment.

Internet

Understanding Microsoft Internet Explorer 5

Microsoft Internet Explorer 5 is a program that allows you to navigate to, open, and view documents. In addition to accessing different kinds of documents on your local computer, you can use Internet Explorer to browse information on the Internet or within an intranet. The **Internet** is a collection of networks that connects computers all over the world. A **network** consists of two or more computers that are connected to share data. The Internet connects millions of computers, using a combination of telephone lines, fiber-optic cables, satellites, and other telecommunications media, as depicted in Figure A-1. The Internet Explorer browser also comes with a set of add-on programs for other common network activities. As assistant to the marketing manager for The Nut Tree, you want to understand the capabilities and functions of Microsoft Internet Explorer 5 and its add-ons, in order to help make your company more successful.

The Internet Explorer Suite includes the following features:

 Internet Explorer, a program known as a **Web browser**, lets you interact with the World Wide Web. The **World Wide Web** (also known as the Web, WWW, and W3) is a vast series of electronic documents called **Web pages** that are linked together over the Internet. Internet Explorer 5 allows you to find, load, view, and interact with Web pages. These pages typically incorporate both text and graphics, as shown in Figure A-2; they also may include multimedia such as sound and video clips.

QuickTip

When you install Internet Explorer 5, you can select the add-ons that you want to install. Thus, you may decide to install only the browser, or the browser along with some or all of the add-ons.

 **FrontPage Express**, an HTML editor for creating Web pages, provides easy-to-use features to modify, format, enhance, and publish Web presentations. **HTML** is a language used to create and structure documents so that they are displayed properly on the Web. Fortunately, FrontPage Express lets you create Web pages without any knowledge of HTML, through its friendly WYSIWYG (What You See Is What You Get) environment.

 Outlook Express, a combined e-mail program and newsgroup reader, allows you to send and receive messages and participate in newsgroup discussions.

 NetMeeting, a real-time audio/video communication program, enables you to speak with and see other people on the Internet or a company intranet. This program also permits you to share and work with drawings, worksheets, and graphics during a conference, regardless of the participants' locations.

 Web Publishing Wizard is a step-by-step way to automate the process of making your Web pages accessible on the Web.

 Windows upgrades include updated versions of some applications that are installed with Windows, as well as new utilities used by both Internet Explorer 5 and your operating system.

FIGURE A-1: Structure of the Internet

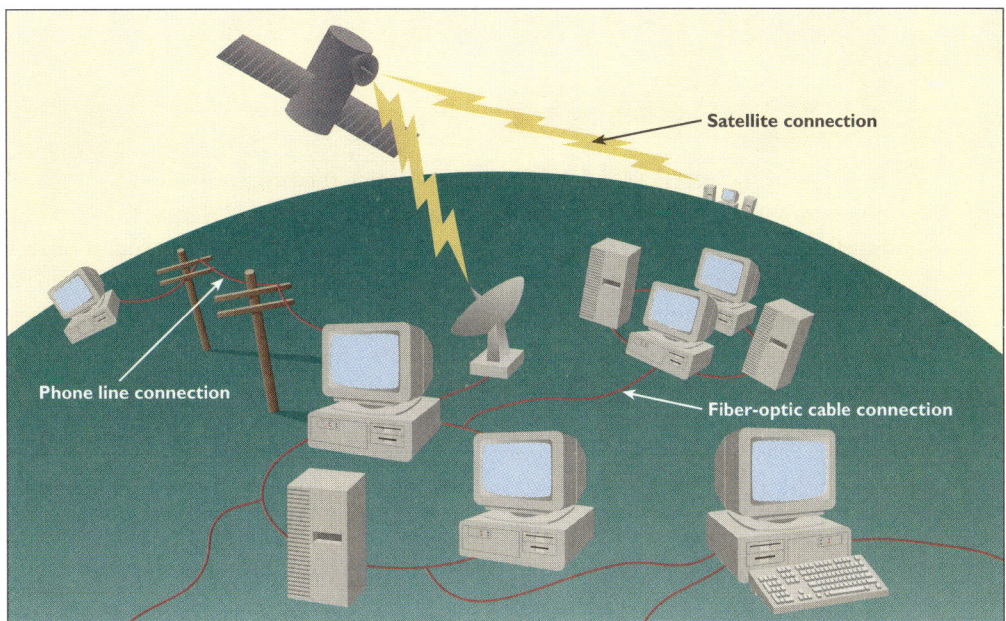

Satellite connection

Phone line connection

Fiber-optic cable connection

FIGURE A-2: Sample World Wide Web page

Understanding intranets

An **intranet** uses the same communications technology as the Internet, but access is available only to the members of a particular company or group. Intranets offer organizations many advantages, such as additional security beyond that available on the Internet, inexpensive and easier installation and maintenance than traditional information systems, and the same familiar Web browser interface that people already use to access information on the Internet. As a consequence, many larger corporations and organizations use intranets to distribute and share information among employees.

Internet

Starting Internet Explorer 5

To begin using Internet Explorer, you simply click the program icon to start it. The exact location and name of the icon may vary on different computers. Hence, the steps you take to start Internet Explorer might differ from those given below. Ask your instructor or technical support person for help if you cannot locate the Internet Explorer icon. ✎ Before you can develop Web-based marketing plans for The Nut Tree's products, you need to start Internet Explorer and investigate its features.

Trouble?

If you do not see the Internet Explorer icon on your taskbar, look for it in the locations shown in Figure A-3. If you do not see the icon in any of these places, ask your instructor or technical support person for help.

1. Locate the **Internet Explorer button** 🅴 on the taskbar

Figure A-3 shows the Internet Explorer button on the taskbar, as well as other common locations. Table A-1 describes other common methods for starting Internet Explorer.

2. Click 🅴

Internet Explorer opens and the home page for this book appears, as shown in Figure A-4. The home page is the first Web page that Internet Explorer loads when you start the program. If you are using the Internet Explorer icon on the desktop, you need to double-click the icon to open Internet Explorer.

3. If Internet Explorer displays the "Welcome—Microsoft Internet Explorer" page, click the **Show this next time you log in check box** to remove the check mark, then click the **Close button**

If your screen differs from the one in Figure A-4, ask your instructor or technical support person for assistance.

TABLE A-1: Common ways to start Internet Explorer 5

method	steps
Taskbar button	Click the Internet Explorer button on the taskbar.
Desktop icon	Double-click the Internet Explorer icon on the desktop.
Start menu	Click the Start button, point to Programs, locate the Internet Explorer icon in the menu system, then click Internet Explorer.

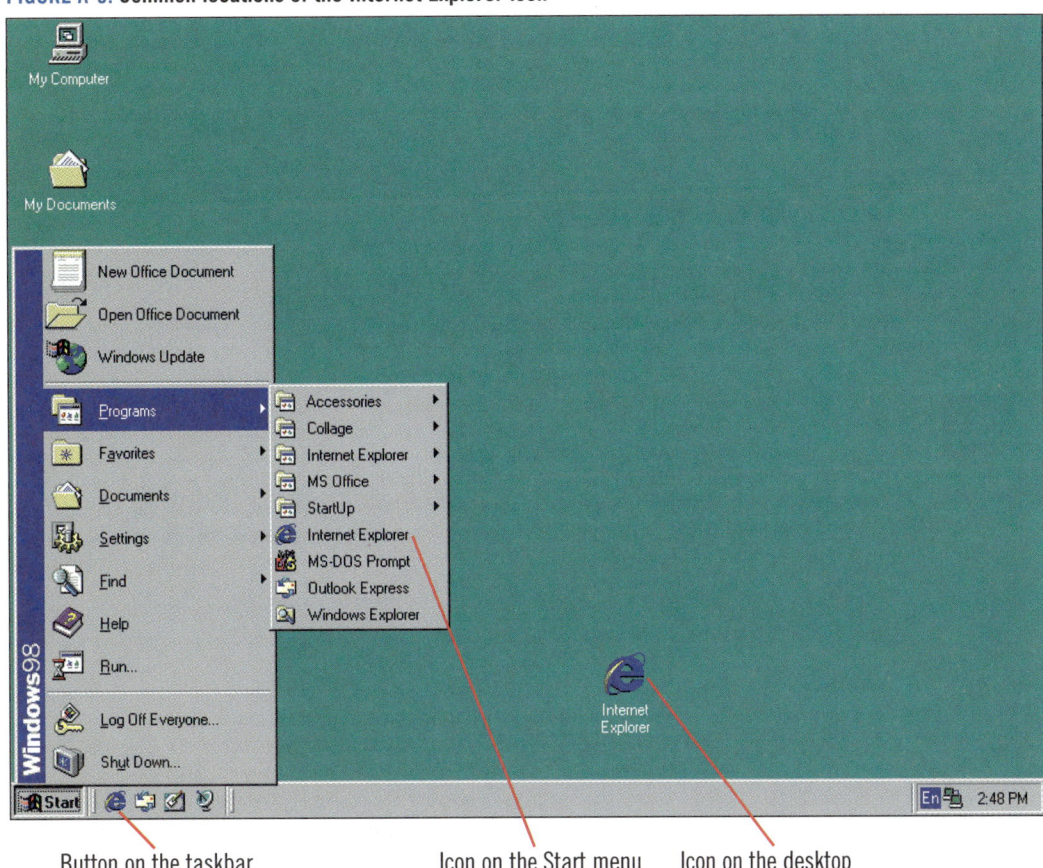

Button on the taskbar   Icon on the Start menu   Icon on the desktop

FIGURE A-4: Home page

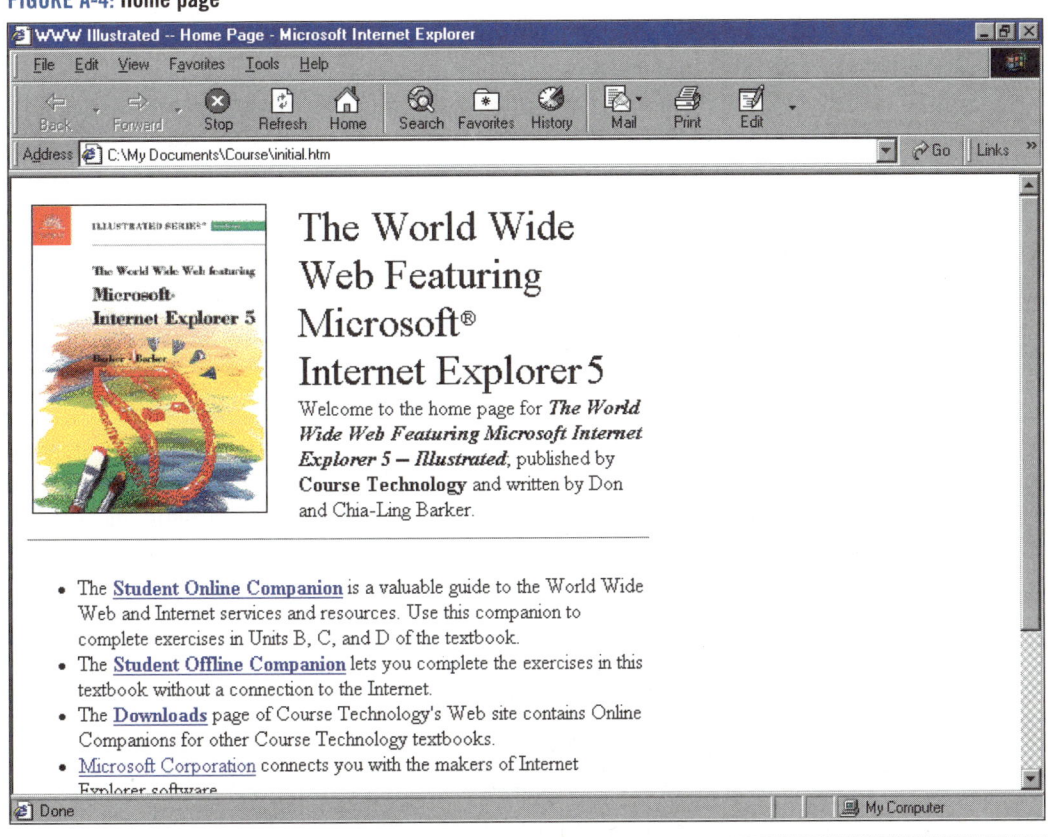

Internet

Investigating the Internet Explorer Window

When you start Internet Explorer, the Explorer application window opens. The screen elements in this window enable you to view, enter, and search for information. To begin your first day on the job at The Nut Tree, you investigate the Internet Explorer environment. Using Figure A-5 as your guide, locate each of the following window elements on your screen:

Details

Trouble?

If your Internet Explorer program window does not cover your entire desktop, click the Maximize button.

 A **Web page** is a specially formatted file designed for use on the World Wide Web. This page can be viewed by anyone with access to the Web. A Web page typically includes text, graphics, and links that, when selected, connect you to other Web pages. It might also include sound and video clips that you can access if your computer has the appropriate hardware and software. The **title bar** displays the title of the current Web page.

 The **menu bar** displays the names of the menus that contain Internet Explorer commands. When you click the name of a menu on the menu bar, Internet Explorer displays a list (menu) of commands from which you can choose.

 The **Standard Buttons toolbar** includes shortcuts to activate frequently used menu commands and navigation aids. It displays the primary navigational buttons used to move around the Web (such as Back, Forward, and Stop). The Standard Buttons toolbar can be customized.

Trouble?

Your Links toolbar may be empty, or may contain different buttons than those in Figure A-5.

 The **Links toolbar** contains a set of buttons that you can customize to quickly access Web pages that you use often.

 The **Radio toolbar**, which is hidden by default, offers tools for listening to Web radio stations from around the world.

 The **Address Bar toolbar** shows the current Web site address and allows the entry or selection of another Web site to view. The **Address text box** displays the address of the page shown in the document window. A **Web address**, or **Uniform Resource Locator (URL)**, is a unique string of text that identifies the location of a Web page on the World Wide Web. You can type a Web page's URL in the Address text box and then click the **Go button** to open the page.

 The **status indicator** (the Internet Explorer or Microsoft Network logo) becomes animated as a new page is loading. When the status indicator stops moving, the page-loading process is complete.

 The **vertical and horizontal scroll bars** enable you to move quickly through a page. The scroll box in each scroll bar indicates your relative position in the page. You may see both, one, or neither of the scroll bars, depending on the dimensions of the page you are viewing.

 The **status bar** displays important information about the current operation, such as the progress of the Web-page-loading process. The center box, called the **progress bar**, visually indicates the status of this process by filling with a blue bar. The right edge shows the general area of the network where the current page resides, such as My Computer (on your local machine) or Internet Zone (on a remote computer).

FIGURE A-5: Elements of the Internet Explorer window

Title bar

Menu bar

Standard Buttons toolbar

Address Bar toolbar

Web address or URL

Web page

Status bar

Status indicator

Go button

Links toolbar

Radio toolbar

Address text box

Scroll box

Document window

Progress bar   Location indicator   Vertical scroll bar

The appearance of toolbars

Internet Explorer 5 takes a unique and useful approach to displaying the toolbars. You can display the sections in a stacked fashion or you can consolidate them into a single row, providing more room for viewing a Web page. By default, Explorer displays the Links and Address Bar toolbars in a single row. To view the Radio toolbar, click View on the Menu bar, point to Toolbars, then click Radio. The Radio toolbar shares the row with the Address and Links toolbars. To expand the toolbars, you can drag the heavy border bar at the bottom of the toolbar down, to fully display one or both of the consolidated toolbars. To redisplay the areas in the consolidated layout, simply drag the heavy toolbar border up. In the consolidated display, the Address Bar, Links toolbar and Radio toolbar share a single row, giving some of them the appearance of a button, by default. You can drag the double-ruled borders between them to change the amount of each toolbar that is exposed.

Internet

Internet

Working with Menus and Toolbars

For many operations, Internet Explorer provides several ways to complete the same task, using either menus or the toolbar. Although the menus in Internet Explorer contain the available commands and options, the toolbars, shown in Figure A-6, offer a quicker and easier way to access frequently used commands. Table A-2 briefly describes the buttons on the Standard Buttons toolbar. ✎ You can use the Explorer window controls to browse for more information on the World Wide Web. Familiarize yourself with these options to learn how they can help you work more efficiently as you market The Nut Tree products online.

QuickTip

Click the list arrow on the right side of the Address text box to display the names of the pages you have visited recently and to display the list of your computer's drives. To revisit a Web page or to open another document from your computer, simply click its name on the list.

1. **Click View on the menu bar, then click Refresh**
   Because your home page hasn't changed, the document window loads and displays the same page, as shown in Figure A-7. Although the page appears the same in this instance, **refreshing**, or reloading, a Web page is an important capability that ensures that you see the most recent version of a Web page. Explorer saves pages that you visit in a file on your computer, called a **cache**, to reduce loading time. The content on the Web changes continually, however, and using Refresh guarantees that you view the most up-to-date information.

2. **Click the Refresh button 🔃 on the Standard toolbar**
   If reloading takes more than a few seconds, the status indicator (the Explorer logo) changes repeatedly. When the status indicator stops switching between images, the page has been successfully reloaded.

3. **Click 🔃 once more, this time quickly clicking the Stop button ⊗ on the toolbar before the home page finishes reloading**
   If you act quickly enough, the home page appears without graphics or other page elements. The Stop button offers a convenient way to halt the lengthy loading process of a page laden with images and other large elements. You will use it often when accessing the Web over a slow Internet connection such as a modem.

4. **Click 🔃 once more to fully load the page**

FIGURE A-6: Internet Explorer toolbars

Standard
Buttons
toolbar

Links toolbar

Address Bar toolbar

Radio toolbar

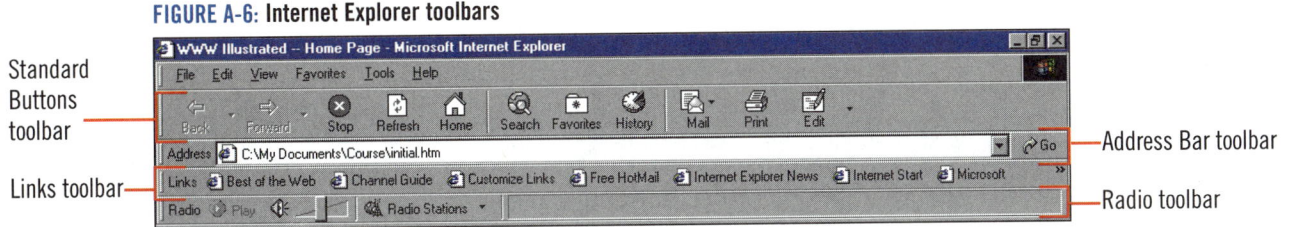

FIGURE A-7: Home page

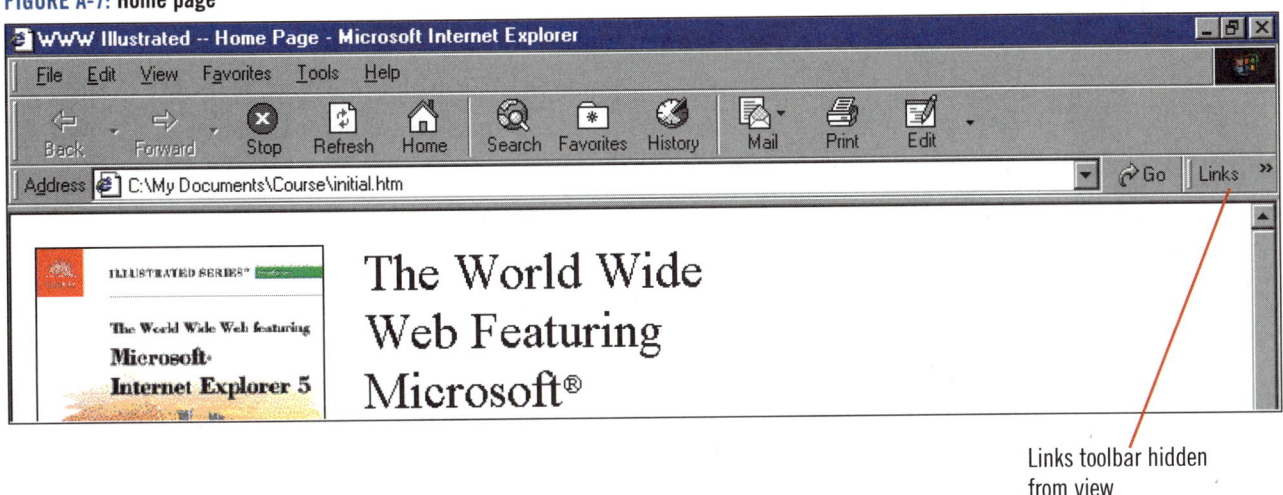

Links toolbar hidden
from view

TABLE A-2: Standard toolbar area options

button	name	description
←	Back	Displays previous page
→	Forward	Displays the next page in the series of pages already viewed
✕	Stop	Halts the page-loading process
⟳	Refresh	Reloads a page
⌂	Home	Displays your home (opening) page
🔍	Search	Allows searches of the Web based on keyword(s)
★	Favorites	Displays a menu of favorite Web sites from which to choose
🕘	History	Displays a menu of previously visited Web sites for quick access
✉	Mail	If installed, allows reading and sending of e-mail and news, along with options for either sending Web page address or the entire page itself in an e-mail message
🖨	Print	Prints current Web page
✎	Edit	Opens the default Web page editor with the current Web page displayed and ready for modification; if Microsoft FrontPage is installed, a different button appears
▤	Discussion	Allows you to post and read messages in discussion groups that are part of some Web pages (Visible only if Office Server Extensions are installed.)

Internet

Moving Around a Web Page

The length of a Web page depends upon the amount of content of the page. Although it is considered wise to keep Web pages short and concise for easy browsing, you will occasionally encounter long pages (such as directories or articles). Internet Explorer provides several convenient methods for moving around Web pages. Table A-3 summarizes the ways in which you can move through a Web page. ✎ Practice moving through your home page, using a variety of the navigation methods available in Internet Explorer.

QuickTip

You can also use the arrow keys and [Page Up] or [Page Down] to display various portions of a Web page in the document window.

1. Click the **scroll down arrow** at the bottom of the vertical scroll bar

The document window scrolls down several lines in the home page to reveal new information at the bottom of the window.

2. Click the **scroll up arrow** at the top of the vertical scroll bar

The document window scrolls up several lines in the home page.

3. Click below the **scroll box** in the vertical scroll bar

The document window scrolls down the length of one window to display the next portion of your home page, stopping at the bottom if less than one window of information remains.

4. Click above the **scroll box** in the vertical scroll bar

The document window scrolls up the length of one window, or back to the top in a short page, to show the previous view of the page.

5. Drag the **scroll box** to the bottom of the vertical scroll bar

The document window displays the bottom of the page, as shown in Figure A-8. Notice that the scroll box has moved to the bottom of the vertical scroll bar, indicating that you have reached the end of the current Web page.

6. Drag the **scroll box** to the top of the vertical scroll bar

The document window displays the top of the page.

7. Press **[Ctrl][End]**

The bottom of the page appears in the document window.

8. Press **[Ctrl][Home]**

The top of the page appears in the document window.

FIGURE A-8: Bottom of the home page

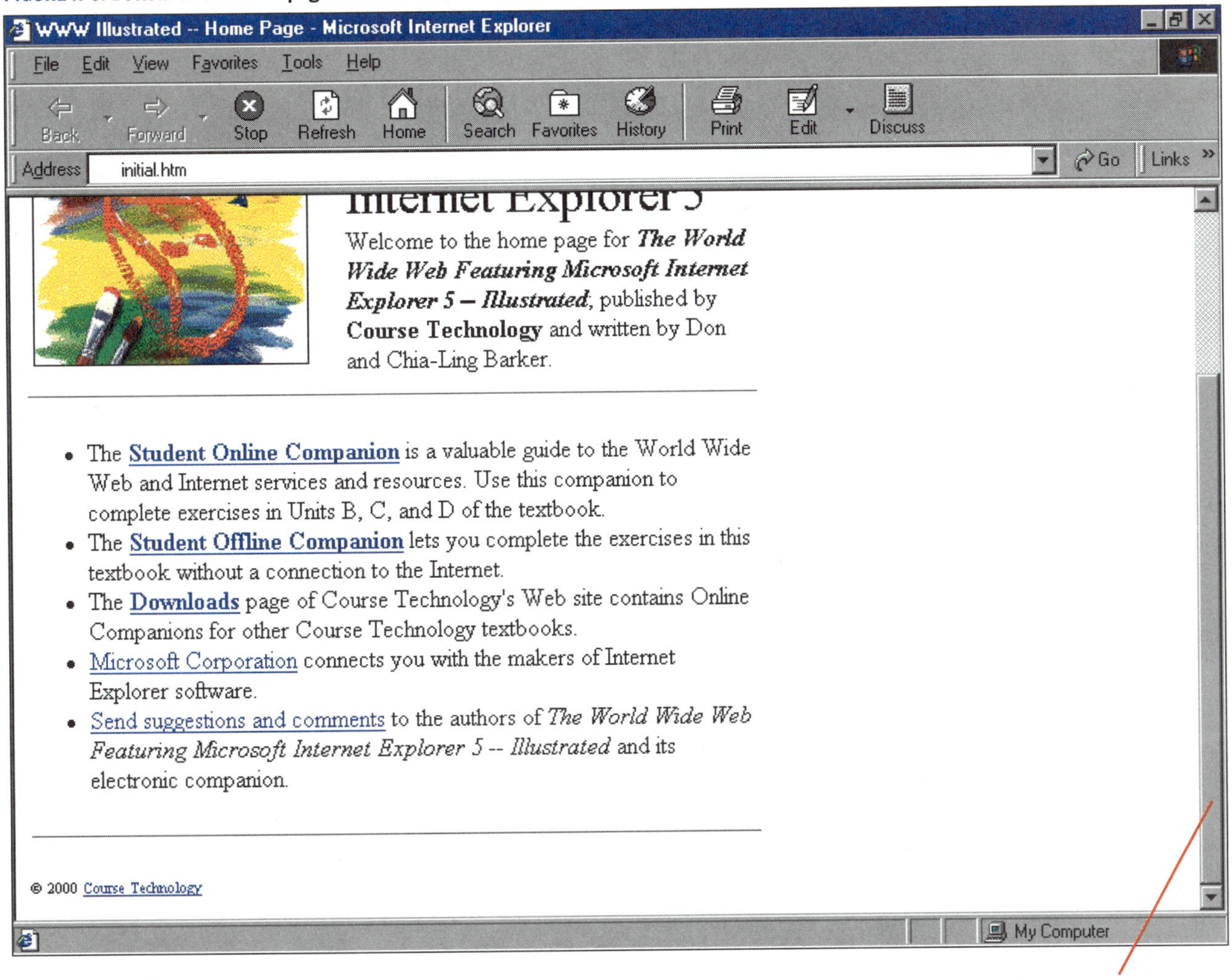

WWW Illustrated -- Home Page - Microsoft Internet Explorer

File   Edit   View   Favorites   Tools   Help

Back   Forward   Stop   Refresh   Home   Search   Favorites   History   Print   Edit   Discuss

Address   initial.htm   Go   Links

Internet Explorer 5

Welcome to the home page for *The World Wide Web Featuring Microsoft Internet Explorer 5 — Illustrated*, published by **Course Technology** and written by Don and Chia-Ling Barker.

- The **Student Online Companion** is a valuable guide to the World Wide Web and Internet services and resources. Use this companion to complete exercises in Units B, C, and D of the textbook.
- The **Student Offline Companion** lets you complete the exercises in this textbook without a connection to the Internet.
- The **Downloads** page of Course Technology's Web site contains Online Companions for other Course Technology textbooks.
- Microsoft Corporation connects you with the makers of Internet Explorer software.
- Send suggestions and comments to the authors of *The World Wide Web Featuring Microsoft Internet Explorer 5 -- Illustrated* and its electronic companion.

© 2000 Course Technology

My Computer

Indicates you have reached the end of the current Web page

TABLE A-3: Methods for moving through a Web page

to move	click or press
Down several lines	Down arrow in the vertical scroll bar or press [↓]
Up several lines	Up arrow in vertical scroll bar or press [↑]
Down one window	Below the scroll box in the vertical scroll bar or press [Page Down]
Up one window	Above the scroll box in the vertical scroll bar or press [Page Up]
To the top of the Web page	[Ctrl][Home]
To the bottom of the Web page	[Ctrl][End]

Internet

Internet

Finding Text

Sometimes you may want to find a specific word or phrase in a Web page because you are seeking information or mention of a particular topic. Scrolling through a Web page and trying to spot text can be a very haphazard and time-consuming process. Fortunately, Internet Explorer provides a Find (on this page) command on the Edit menu to automate this process. You are searching for information on how to market products on the Web, so use the Find (on this page) command to search for occurrences of the word "Web."

QuickTip

You can also press [Ctrl][F] to open the Find dialog box.

1. **Make sure your home page is open, click Edit on the menu bar, then click Find (on this page)**
   The Find dialog box opens, as shown in Figure A-9. Table A-4 lists all of the Find dialog box options.

2. **Click in the Find what text box, then type Web**
   The word "Web" appears in the text box.

Trouble?

If you do not see the word "Web" highlighted on the page, reposition the Find dialog box so that the highlighted term is visible.

3. **Click the Find Next button in the dialog box**
   The document window changes to show the portion of the page containing the first instance of "Web."

4. **Click the Find Next button in the dialog box again**
   The second occurrence of "Web" in this page appears highlighted in the document window. You may need to reposition the Find dialog box to see the next instance of "Web" that is highlighted on the Web page.

5. **Click the Find Next button again**
   Yet another instance of "Web" is found.

6. **Continue to click the Find Next button until you receive the message "Finished searching the document," then click OK in the dialog box**
   Internet Explorer has now searched the entire page from top to bottom.

7. **Click the Cancel button in the dialog box to close it**
   The last instance of "Web" remains highlighted after the Find dialog box is closed.

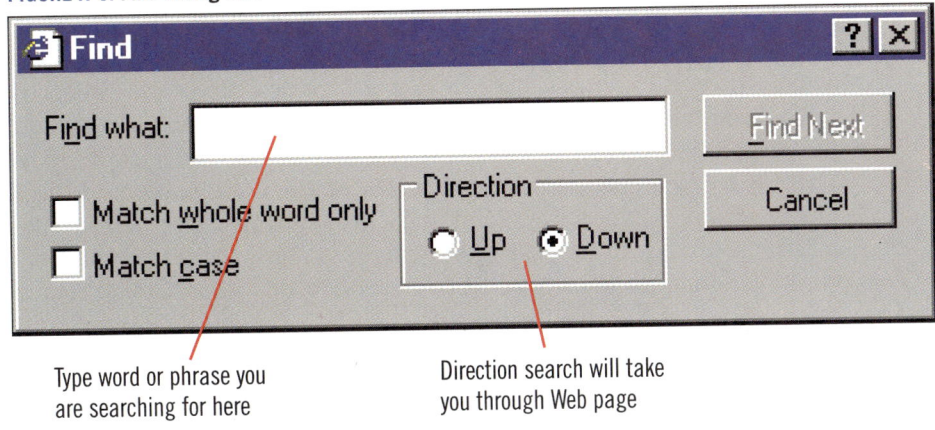

Type word or phrase you
are searching for here

Direction search will take
you through Web page

TABLE A-4: Find dialog box options

option	description
Find what text box	Allows the entry of keywords for which to search
Find Next button	Locates and highlights the next occurrence of text in a Web page that matches the entry in the Find what text box
Cancel button	Closes the Find dialog box
Match whole word only check box	Skips finding words that may contain the keyword (for example, Webcasting) and displays only occurrences of the word by itself (for example, Web)
Match case check box	Causes Internet Explorer to search for text that exactly matches the capitalization used in the Find what text box
Up option button	Searches the Web page from the insertion point up for a match to the entry in the Find what text box
Down option button	Searches the Web page from the insertion point down for a match to the entry in the Find what text box

Internet

Internet

Getting Help

Microsoft Internet Explorer includes a Help system that can provide information and instructions on the features and commands you are using in the Explorer browser and the other Internet Explorer components (such as FrontPage Express). This system is a valuable resource when you are uncertain how to accomplish a task or encounter unexpected results while using Internet Explorer. ▬▬ As the new assistant to the marketing manager for The Nut Tree, you want to familiarize yourself with the Help information available in Microsoft Internet Explorer. Use the Contents and Index command on the Help menu to view information about this program.

Steps 1234

1. **Click Help on the menu bar**

   The Help menu opens, displaying several options including Contents and Index, Tip of the Day, For Netscape Users, Tour, Online Support, Send Feedback, Repair, and About Internet Explorer. The Contents and Index command provides specific information on Internet Explorer. Tip of the Day gives a random hint on using Internet Explorer's features effectively. For Netscape Users provides helpful information for users familiar with Netscape Navigator, a Web browser similar to Internet Explorer. Tour offers a guided tour of Web basics and the use of Explorer. Online Support allows you to search the Microsoft Web site for specific information about Internet Explorer. Send Feedback allows you to contact Microsoft with a comment or question. Repair allows you to fix problems with your Internet Explorer installation. About Internet Explorer displays the program's version and copyright information.

   Trouble?

   If an error dialog box appears when you select a Help command, it probably indicates that you are not currently connected to the Internet. Although the Contents and Index features are available offline (locally), the other Help menu options require you to be online (that is, connected to the Internet).

2. **Click Contents and Index**

   The Internet Explorer Help dialog box opens, as shown in Figure A-10. Table A-5 describes the options in the Help Topics dialog box. For now, you simply want to investigate the basic features of Explorer.

3. **Click the Customizing your browser Contents item, then click the item Turn off graphics to display all Web pages faster from the list that appears below it**

   A description of how to make Web pages open faster by turning off graphics appears in the right portion of the window, as shown in Figure A-11.

4. **Scan the information displayed in the right section of the window**

5. **When you have finished reviewing the topic, click the Close button in the upper-right corner of the Help window to close it**

   Internet Explorer appears on your desktop, with your home page displayed in the document window.

FIGURE A-10: Internet Explorer Help window

Index tab

Contents tab

Currently selected
Help topic

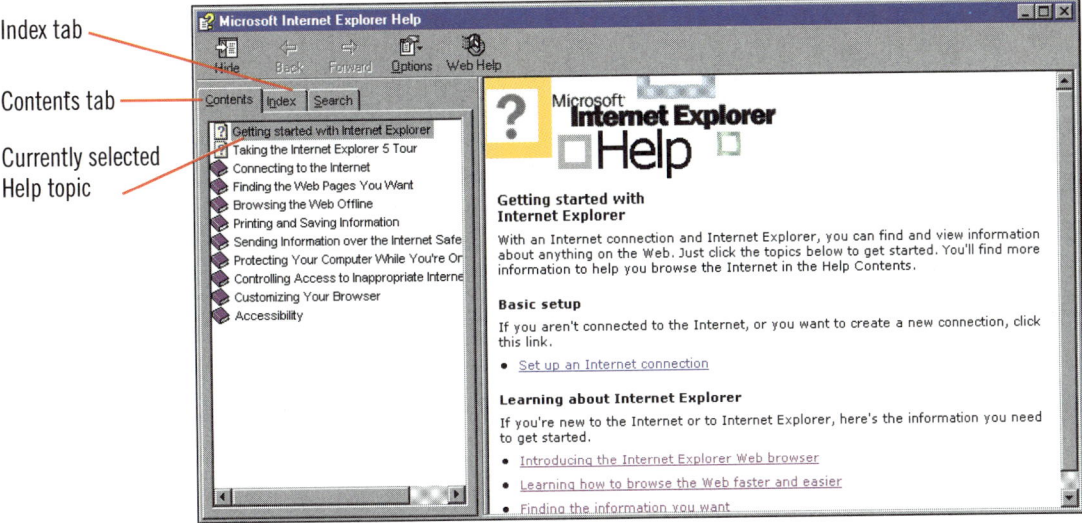

FIGURE A-11: Information on browsing the Web faster

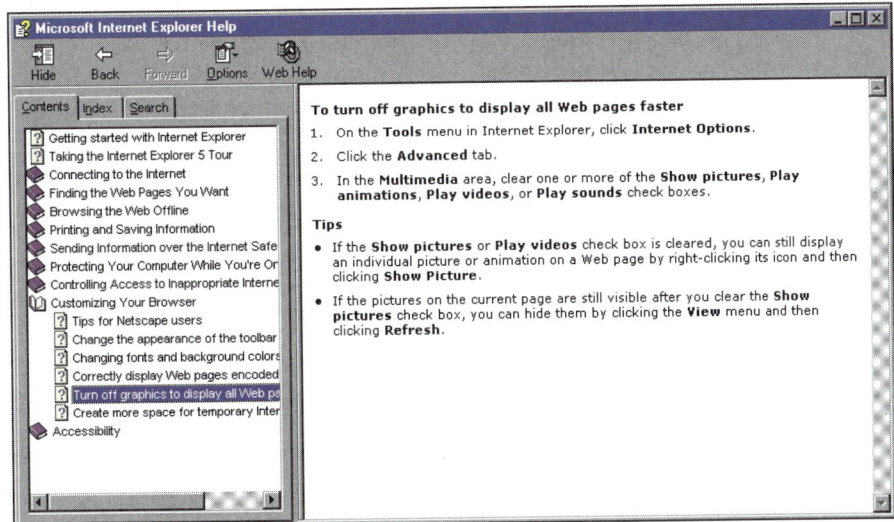

TABLE A-5: Descriptions of the Help options

command	provides
Contents tab	Offers a variety of topics about Explorer to investigate
Index tab	Allows the search of Help documents by topic
Search tab	Allows the search of Help documents by keyword
Display button	On the Index and Search tabs, opens a window displaying information on the chosen topic
Hide button	Removes the Contents and Index tabs from view
Show button	Makes the Contents and Index tabs visible
Back button	Allows a return to a previously viewed Help window
Forward button	Allows a return to next document in series of Help windows already viewed
Options button	Opens menu of additional options for working with the Help window
Web Help button	Provides a link to additional Help resources online

Internet

Printing a Web Page

Internet Explorer allows you to print the current Web page (that is, the one displayed in your document window). Printing a Web page can be useful if you find information that you'd like to review later, away from your computer. It also allows you to easily share information you find on the Web with friends and associates. ➤ Melissa Shea, marketing manager for The Nut Tree, has never used the Internet or the World Wide Web. She has asked to see a printout of what a home page looks like. Use the Print dialog box to print two copies of your home page—one for Melissa and one for your records.

Steps 1234

1. **Click File on the menu bar, then click Print**

   The Print dialog box opens, as shown in Figure A-12. Table A-6 describes the Internet Explorer printing options.

2. **Double-click the Number of copies text box, then type 2**

   The Print dialog box is now set to print two copies. If you accidentally entered a different number of copies, repeat Step 2 to correct the mistake. (*Note*: This number of copies becomes the default number to print until you exit Internet Explorer or change the number.)

3. **Make sure your printer is turned on, is ready to print, and contains paper**

4. **Click OK**

   The Print dialog box closes and the current Web page prints.

Trouble?

If you are not connected to a printer, or if the printer fails to work, ask your technical support person or instructor for assistance.

FIGURE A-12: Print dialog box

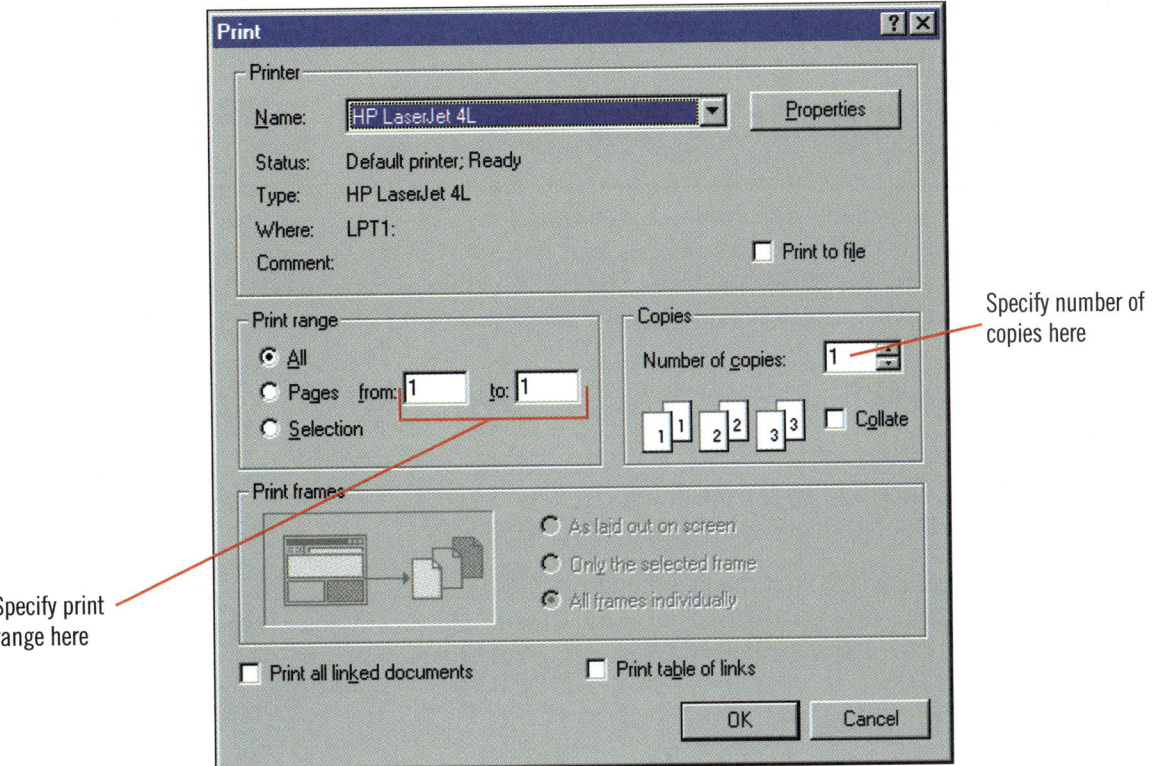

Specify number of copies here

Specify print range here

TABLE A-6: Printing options

options	description
Printer	Displays information about the active printer *Name* indicates the printer to use *Status* reveals the readiness of the printer *Type* displays the brand and model of the active printer *Where* shows the destination of the print job *Comment* displays available information on printing *Properties* provides access to the settings of the active printer *Print to file* sends a print job to a file instead of to a printer
Print range	Indicates the pages to print *All* prints the entire document *Pages* prints only specified pages *Selection* prints selected portions of the document
Copies	Indicates the number and order of copies to print *Number of copies* specifies how many copies to print *Collate* prints multiple copies of the document in sequence
Print frames	Displays options for how frames are printed *As laid out on screen* prints all frames together on the page as the screen displays them *Only the selected frame* prints the current frame by itself *All frames individually* prints each frame independently of the others
Print all linked documents	Prints the selected area as well as the contents of each page for which a link exists in the selected area
Print table of links	Prints the selected area as well as a table listing all links located in the selected area

Internet

Exiting Internet Explorer

In many other Windows programs, you need to save documents before exiting. However, a Web browser simply displays documents and allows the user to interact with them; it does not make changes to Web pages themselves. Therefore, you can close Internet Explorer at any time without losing data. ✎ You have completed your first day as assistant to the marketing manager for The Nut Tree. Exit Internet Explorer before leaving the office.

Steps 1 2 3 4

1. **Click File on the menu bar**
   The File menu opens, as shown in Figure A-13.

2. **Click Close on the File menu**
   The Internet Explorer program window closes and you return to Windows. Table A-7 describes alternate ways to close Internet Explorer.

TABLE A-7: Common methods of closing Internet Explorer

method	procedure
Menu bar	Click File on the menu bar, then click Close
Title bar buttons	Click the Close button on the title bar
Taskbar	Right-click the Internet Explorer program window icon on the taskbar, then click Close

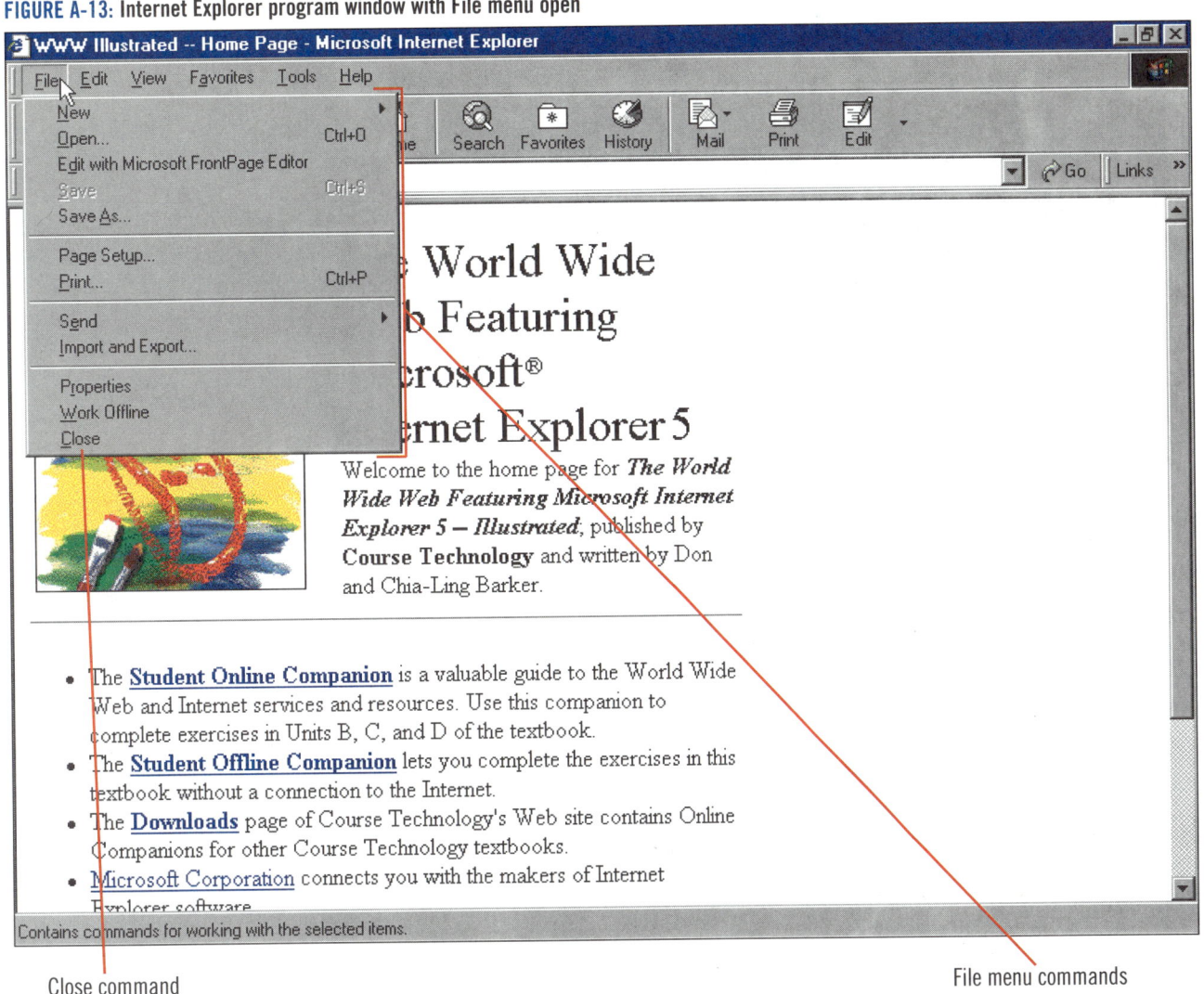

Close command

File menu commands

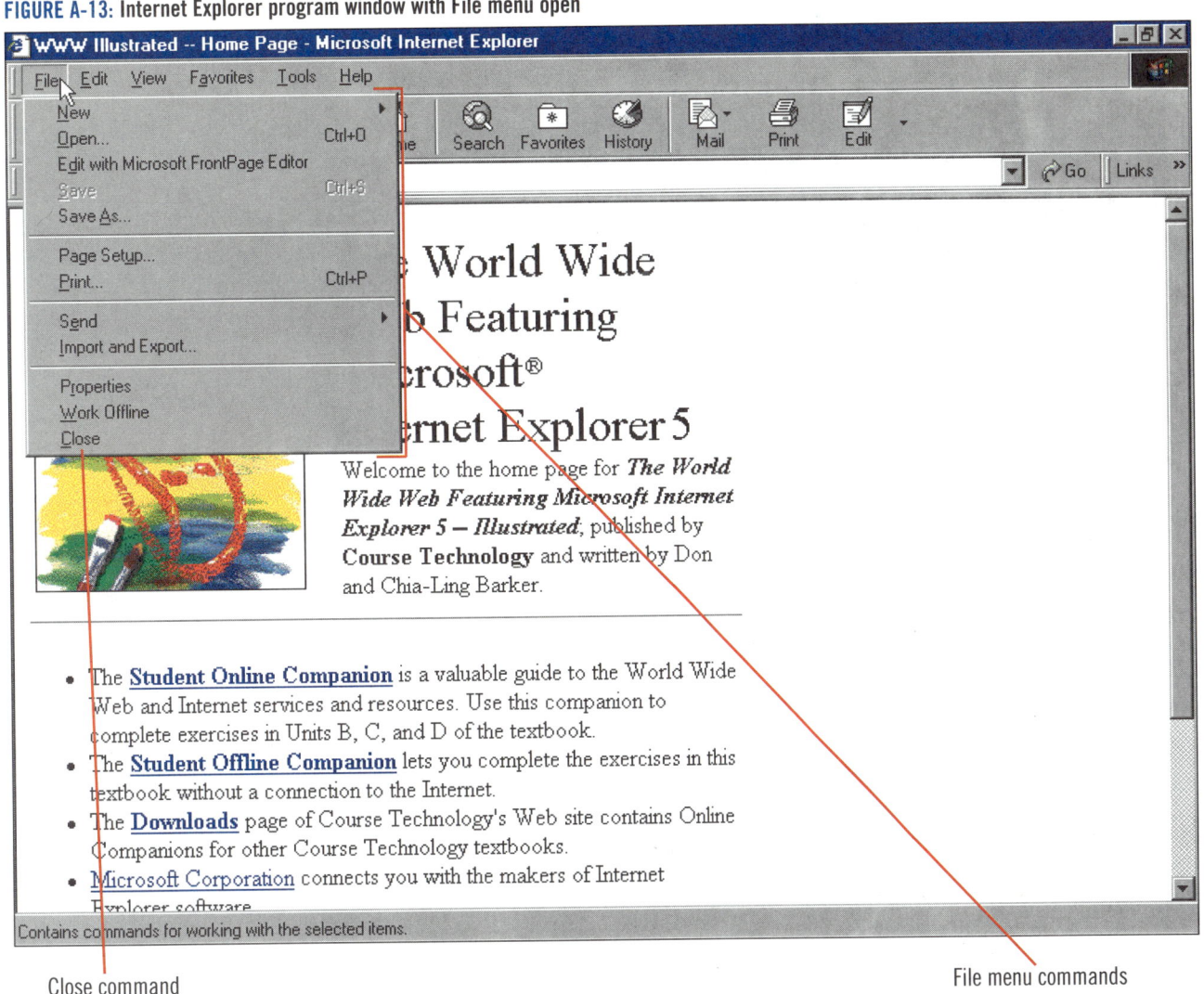

Opening, switching, and closing multiple instances of Internet Explorer

You can use the New, Window command on the File menu to open another instance of the Internet Explorer program. Each **instance** is a separate Internet Explorer window, complete with all toolbars and menus, in which you can navigate independently. Additionally, some hyperlinks open linked Web pages in new Internet Explorer instances, while leaving the referencing page displayed in the original instance. The taskbar allows you to switch between these different instances. To close an instance of Explorer, use any of the methods described in Table A-7 for the instance that you want to close.

Internet

Practice

► Concepts Review

Label each of the elements of the Internet Explorer program window in Figure A-14.

FIGURE A-14

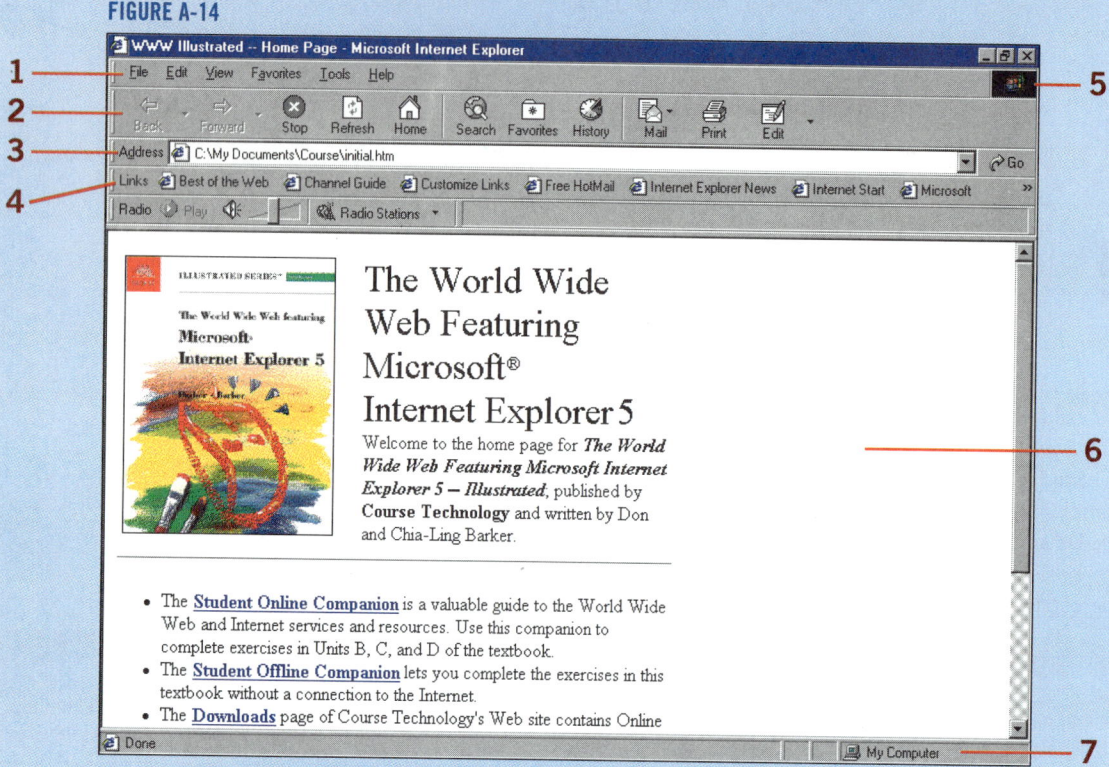

Match each of the terms below with the statement that best describes its function.

8. Standard Buttons toolbar   **a.** Displays a Web page

9. Scroll bar   **b.** Indicates Internet Explorer is loading a page

10. Document window   **c.** Contains shortcuts to menu commands

11. Address text box   **d.** Indicates the address of the current page

12. Status indicator   **e.** Contains controls for moving through a document

Select the best answer from the list of choices.

13. **Which is NOT a component of Microsoft Internet Explorer?**
    - **a.** Internet Explorer
    - **b.** FrontPage Express
    - **c.** NetMeeting
    - **d.** Messenger

14. **A Web browser lets you**
  a. Create Web pages.
  b. Explore binary files on your hard disk.
  c. View pages on the Web.
  d. Browse non-ASCII files at remote sites.

15. **To view another part of a Web page**
  a. Click the Relocate button on the toolbar.
  b. Move the scroll box in the scroll bar.
  c. Drag the toolbar.
  d. Select the Leap command from the Navigate menu.

16. **To go to the top of a document**
  a. Drag the scroll box to the top of the scroll bar.
  b. Press [Ctrl][Top].
  c. Click the Home button on the toolbar.
  d. Double-click the scroll bar.

17. **To find words in a Web page**
  a. Click the Find button.
  b. Press [Ctrl][F].
  c. Click the Find in command on the Edit menu.
  d. Double-click the Location toolbar.

18. **You can access Internet Explorer Help by**
  a. Clicking Help on the menu bar.
  b. Pressing [F2].
  c. Clicking the Help button on the toolbar.
  d. Pressing [Alt][Help].

19. **Which key(s) do you press to move down a Web page?**
  a. [End]
  b. [Page Down]
  c. [Shift][End]
  d. [Enter][End]

20. **You can print a document in Internet Explorer in any of the following ways, except by**
  a. Clicking the Print button on the toolbar.
  b. Clicking File, clicking Print, and then clicking OK.
  c. Clicking File, clicking Print Preview, and then clicking Print.
  d. Pressing [Alt][P] and then [Enter].

21. **The Standard Buttons toolbar lets you do all of the following, except**
  a. Print a Web page.
  b. Search the Web.
  c. See how much of a Web page has loaded.
  d. See a list of your favorite Web sites.

Internet

22. Your home page is
  a. A Web page detailing information about your computer.
  b. The initial Web page that Internet Explorer loads whenever you start the program.
  c. A page you must create yourself.
  d. A Web page devoted to the realty business.

23. URL stands for
  a. Universal Requester List.
  b. Uniform Resource List.
  c. Uniform Resource Locator.
  d. Universal Regional Locator.

24. You can exit Internet Explorer by
  a. Clicking Internet Explorer's Close button.
  b. Clicking Done on the File menu.
  c. Clicking Done on the Go menu.
  d. All of the above.

Skills Review

1. Start Internet Explorer and identify elements of the program window.
  a. Make sure the computer is on and Windows is running.
  b. Click the Internet Explorer button on the taskbar.
  c. Without referring to the lesson material, identify the toolbar areas, the Address Bar, the menu bar, the scroll bars, the location text box, the status indicator, and the progress bar in the Internet Explorer program window.

2. Move around the document window.
  a. Click the scroll down arrow in the vertical scroll bar twice.
  b. Click the scroll up arrow on the vertical scroll bar twice.
  c. Click below the scroll box in the vertical scroll bar.
  d. Click above the scroll box in the vertical scroll bar.
  e. Drag the scroll box to the bottom of the vertical scroll bar.

3. Find text.
  a. Click the Find (on this page) command on the Edit menu to open the Find dialog box.
  b. Use the dialog box to locate each instance of the word "Internet" in your home page.
  c. Double-check your results by searching the document with the Up option button in the Direction area of the Find dialog box.
  d. Close the Find dialog box.

4. Explore Internet Explorer Help.
  a. Click Help on the menu bar.
  b. Click the Contents and Index command on the Help menu.
  c. Click the Index tab, and then if necessary, click in the text box above the list that appears.
  d. Type "Viewing Web pages," click one of the topics that appears in the box below, then click the Display button.
  e. Read the information displayed on the right side of the screen, then close the Help window.

5. Print a Web page and exit Internet Explorer.

  a. If necessary, click the Home button on the toolbar.

  b. Scroll to the bottom of your home page, then click the "Course Technology" link.

  c. When the Course Technology home page finishes loading in the document window, click File on the menu bar, then click Print.

  d. To print only the first page of this Web document, click the Pages option button in the Print range area of the Print dialog box.

  e. Press [Tab], type "1" in the To text box, if necessary, then click OK.

  f. When the page is printed, click File on the menu bar, then click Close.

▶ Independent Challenges

1. Write a short essay on what you hope to learn from this book. Include a description of how you think the World Wide Web will help you in your academic or professional life. You can use any word processor to write and print this essay. If you are unfamiliar with a word processor, use Notepad, a simple text processor included with Microsoft Windows in the Accessories program group.

2. You are working with a public service group that encourages people to research products they plan to buy, and the businesses that make them, before making a purchase. You have read about the Web and electronic commerce, and want to find out how this can help your agency fulfill its mission. Use your library to find several recent articles on how the World Wide Web is affecting businesses, including at least one article on electronic commerce. Write a brief summary of the articles. You can use any word processor to write and print the summary. If you are unfamiliar with a word processor, use Notepad, a simple text processor included with Microsoft Windows in the Accessories program group.

Visual Workshop

Use the skills you learned in this unit to display the "Using secure Web sites for transactions" topic in the Help window, as shown in Figure A-15. Print a copy of this page.

FIGURE A-15

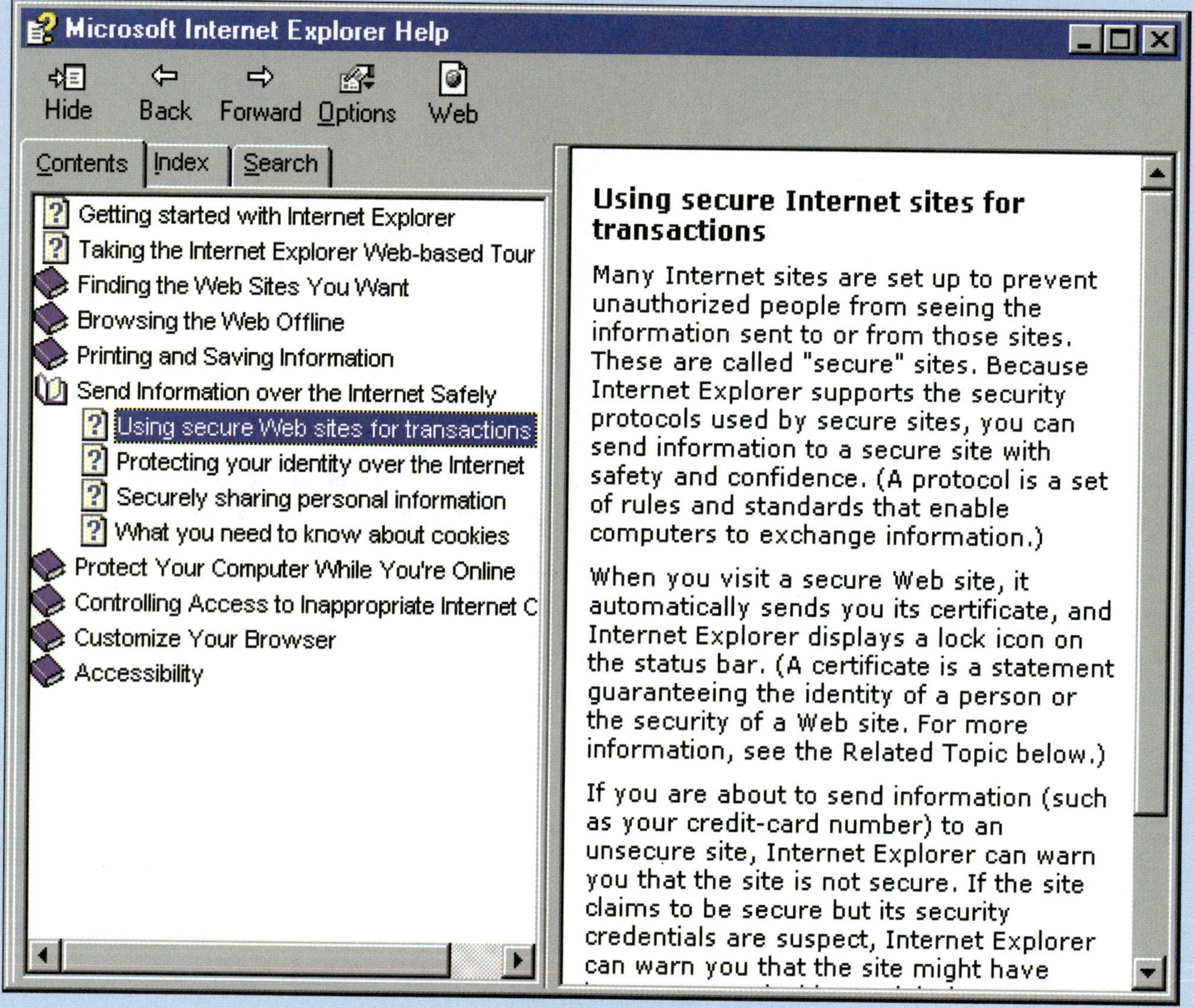

Microsoft Internet Explorer Help

Hide   Back   Forward   Options   Web

Contents | Index | Search

- Getting started with Internet Explorer
- Taking the Internet Explorer Web-based Tour
- Finding the Web Sites You Want
- Browsing the Web Offline
- Printing and Saving Information
- Send Information over the Internet Safely
  - Using secure Web sites for transactions
  - Protecting your identity over the Internet
  - Securely sharing personal information
  - What you need to know about cookies
- Protect Your Computer While You're Online
- Controlling Access to Inappropriate Internet C
- Customize Your Browser
- Accessibility

Using secure Internet sites for transactions

Many Internet sites are set up to prevent unauthorized people from seeing the information sent to or from those sites. These are called "secure" sites. Because Internet Explorer supports the security protocols used by secure sites, you can send information to a secure site with safety and confidence. (A protocol is a set of rules and standards that enable computers to exchange information.)

When you visit a secure Web site, it automatically sends you its certificate, and Internet Explorer displays a lock icon on the status bar. (A certificate is a statement guaranteeing the identity of a person or the security of a Web site. For more information, see the Related Topic below.)

If you are about to send information (such as your credit-card number) to an unsecure site, Internet Explorer can warn you that the site is not secure. If the site claims to be secure but its security credentials are suspect, Internet Explorer can warn you that the site might have

Navigating
the Web

Objectives

- ► **Understand hyperlinks and URLs**
- ► **Find, start, and stop hyperlinks**
- ► **Move backward and forward**
- ► **View history**
- ► **Use Favorites**
- ► **Work with frames**
- ► **Customize the Toolbar**
- ► **Enter a URL**

Once you are familiar with Internet Explorer's toolbars, menus, dialog boxes, and Help system, you are ready to navigate the Web. This unit will introduce the basic techniques for moving between Web pages using Internet Explorer. In addition to using different methods to open a Web page, you will return to pages you have already viewed and add a page to your list of favorite pages for easy access. ✎ As assistant to the marketing manager for The Nut Tree, you believe that the Web could be a significant resource for marketing and selling the firm's products. Before making any recommendations to your marketing manager, Melissa Shea, you want to become more adept at moving around the Web.

Understanding Hyperlinks and URLs

Like a conventional reference resource, such as an encyclopedia, the World Wide Web is composed of a large number of pages filled with all sorts of information. Like the cross-references at the end of an encyclopedia entry, a Web page can contain hypertext links to refer users to related Web pages. **Hypertext links**, more commonly known as **hyperlinks** or just **links**, are Web page elements that you can click to open other Web pages. You can use hyperlinks to follow a topic from page to page through the Web, without regard to where or in what order the pages reside. To distinguish them from the other text in a Web page, hyperlinks are highlighted in a special color and underlined. Figure B-1 shows a Web page featuring hyperlinks to other pages on the same Web site. If any of the descriptions interested you, you could simply click on the hyperlink, and your Web browser would locate and load the indicated Web page. Each Web page has an address within the World Wide Web, called a **Uniform Resource Locator**, or **URL** for short. Internet Explorer displays the URL for the current page in the Address bar. For example, the URL for the Web page shown in Figure B-1 is http://www.powells.com/. You have already noticed a few URLs in articles you have read about the Web. Before you begin working on the Web, you are interested in knowing what the information in a URL means. After a bit of research, you discover that several common components make up each URL.

 Each URL for a page on the World Wide Web begins with the acronym HTTP. **HTTP** (Hypertext Transfer Protocol) is the Web's communications standard. It ensures that different computers communicate in the same language when sending and receiving Web pages. This acronym is always followed by a colon and two forward slashes (http://) to indicate that the Web page is located on a remote Web server. A **Web server** consists of a computer or a network of computers that stores Web pages and makes them available on the Web.

 The name of a Web site typically begins with the letters "www" (for example, www.powells.com), signifying that the location is part of the World Wide Web. The remainder of the site name (for example, powells.com) is called the **domain name**.

 The first component of the domain name (for example, powells) usually stands for the name of the institution that owns the site.

 The final three letters, the **global**, or **top-level domain** or **extension** (for example, .com), indicate the kind of site or institution with which you are dealing. In this case, .com indicates that this site is a commercial one. Table B-1 briefly describes the top-level domain extensions in current usage, as well as new extensions that have been proposed. InterNIC, the private company in charge of registering Internet domain names, has suggested the addition of the new top-level domains, but it's uncertain if or when they will actually be implemented. Each extension is suggested for use by a specific type of organization; however, any group may register a domain name using any extension.

URL

Hyperlink

Web page

TABLE B-1: Global domains

status	global domain	description
In use	.com	Commercial sites
	.edu	Educational institutions
	.mil	Military
	.net	Network organizations (computer services that connect remote computers)
	.org	Not-for-profit organizations
	.gov	Government agencies, departments, and institutions
Proposed	.firm	Commercial sites
	.shop	Business sites selling products
	.web	Entities involved in Web-related activities (for example, an Internet service provider)
	.arts	Arts and cultural organizations
	.rec	Recreation-related groups
	.info	Information service providers
	.nom	Personal sites

CLUES TO USE

Graphical hyperlinks

Hyperlinks to other Web pages can appear as graphics as well as text. Just as with text hyperlinks, you can click a linked graphic to open a new Web page. Different parts of a single graphic can also contain links to separate pages. For example, a Web page might display a picture of the solar system, showing the sun and the nine planets. Each planet could serve as a link to a page containing information about that planet. Such a graphic containing multiple links is known as an **image map**. Because graphical hyperlinks are easy to understand and use, many Web sites use image maps to simplify navigation.

Internet

Unit **B**

Internet

Finding, Starting, and Stopping Hyperlinks

To make them easily recognizable, text hyperlinks are always highlighted in a different color than the rest of the text on a Web page. Once you select a link, it often changes color to indicate that you have chosen it. Usually, unselected, or **unfollowed**, hyperlinks are blue by default, while hyperlinks that have previously been selected, or **followed**, are purple. By changing the color of a link, Internet Explorer provides a clear marker to help you keep track of your travels on the World Wide Web. Because the link color setting can be changed on individual computers, as well as by the creator of each Web page, hyperlinks may not always appear in the default colors.

To select a link in a Web page, simply click it. Internet Explorer will then attempt to locate and open the page, using its URL address. Because the Web runs over the Internet, which has thousands of sites connected by thousands of networks, things can sometimes go wrong when you try to load a page. If your browser seems to be taking a very long time to locate and/or load a page, you can interrupt the operation by clicking the Stop button on the toolbar. Begin your quest for information on using the Web as a marketing tool by selecting a link.

QuickTip

If you are using the Student Offline Companion, read the Clues to Use box on p. B-5.

1. Start Internet Explorer, make sure the window is maximized, scroll through your home page until you locate the link **Student Online Companion**; or, if you are working offline, locate the **Student Offline Companion** link, then position the mouse pointer over the link
   Notice that when you move the mouse pointer over the link, its shape changes from an arrow ⤢ to a hand ⤒. This transformation also indicates that an image is a hyperlink.

Trouble?

If your home page does not contain the Student Online Companion link, check with your instructor or technical support person.

2. Click the **Student Online Companion** link or the **Student Offline Companion** link
   After a moment, the status indicator stops moving, and the document window displays the Student Online Companion, as shown in Figure B-2. This page provides an extensive guide to sites on the Web and is designed for use with this textbook. You want to select a link from this page that will lead you to Web pages providing information on other companies selling products and services on the Web.

3. Scroll through the Web page until you reach the heading **Exploring the Web**, then click the folder to the left of the heading
   A list of related topics appears beneath the heading.

4. Click the folder to the left of **Exploring electronic commerce**
   The Web page displays a list of links to Web sites related to electronic commerce.

QuickTip

If you click the Stop button too soon, your document window may remain empty. Click the Refresh button on the toolbar to restart the loading process, and then wait until the page begins to appear before clicking the Stop button. If you receive an error message, click OK and try this step again.

5. Click the **E-Commerce Watch** link; as the new Web page begins to load, click the **Stop button** ⊗ on the toolbar
   Internet Explorer halts the process of finding and loading the linked page. When you click the Stop button, the document window displays the portion of the new page that Internet Explorer was able to load before the loading operation was halted. Internet Explorer will continue to display the current page in the document window until a new page begins loading.

6. Click the **Refresh button** ⟳ to load the page fully, then review the page contents

FIGURE B-2: Student Online Companion page for this book

Tips for users of the Student Offline Companion

If you are using the Student Offline Companion with this text, you are working with Web pages that are stored on your local drive or network rather than on the Internet. The Student Offline Companion contains the Web pages needed to complete all of the lessons and most of the end-of-unit exercises for this book. To keep the Offline Companion to a reasonable size, only those hyperlinks that are necessary to complete the lessons or exercises are active on each Web page. Because it is designed to simulate the experience of working online, the heading on the Offline Companion home page says "Student Online Companion."

The pages with which you are working are located on a local disk drive. As a result, the URLs in the Address bar on your screen differ from those in the book. Your screen shows a local drive address (simply a filename) for each Web page loaded, rather than an

HTTP address (beginning with "http://"). For instance, in Figure B-2, the address displayed for users of the Offline Companion is "file:///C|/Offline/Course/index.htm" (or a similar directory and drive location), rather than the URL shown in the figure.

In addition, the URLs that the book instructs you to type differ if you are using the Student Offline Companion. In the lessons, alternate addresses are provided for Offline Companion users; for end-of-unit exercises, your instructor can supply you with replacement addresses for those sites you need to access. If possible, however, you should complete the end-of-unit exercises online rather than offline, so that you can gain experience actually working on the Internet and thoroughly explore the resources available on the World Wide Web.

Moving Backward and Forward

Internet Explorer makes it easy to navigate backward and forward through Web pages you have previously viewed. As you navigate among Web pages, Internet Explorer maintains a list of the URLs you have opened, in the order you have viewed them. You can click the Back button on the toolbar to display the page immediately before the current page in the list. If you have used the Back button to return to an earlier page, and then want to move to a later page, you can use the Forward button to move forward in the series of pages you have viewed. Melissa Shea was impressed by the Web marketing resources you found in the previous lesson. Now that you have found a source for this information, you need to find out how to put The Nut Tree's company and product information onto the Web. Use the Back and Forward buttons to return to the Student Online Companion page and look for another link that may provide the information you want.

Steps 1234

1. Click the **Back button** ⇐ on the toolbar once
The previously viewed page appears in your document window, with the directory lists restored to their unexpanded form.

2. Click ⇐ until it grays out
Your home page appears in the document window. As shown in Figure B-3, the Back button is now grayed out to indicate that you have reached the first page viewed and that this button is temporarily unavailable for use.

3. Click the **Forward button** ⇒ once
The Student Online Companion page appears, as shown in Figure B-4. Notice that the Back and Forward buttons are not grayed out.

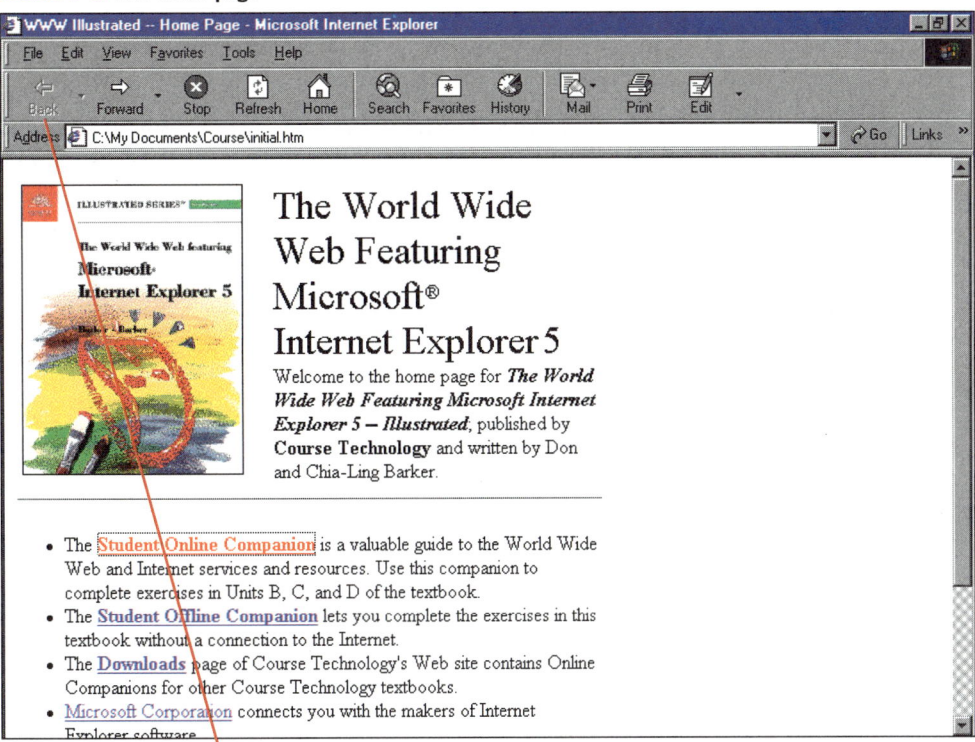

The Back button is grayed out
to indicate it is inactive

The Back and Forward
buttons are both active

Internet

Viewing History

Internet Explorer offers another way to move among previously selected Web pages—the History command. Instead of using the Back and Forward buttons to search for a previously viewed page, you can go straight to that page by clicking the History button and then selecting the name of any previously visited page. Use the History command to review the Web pages you have already visited and to make sure you didn't overlook anything of value.

Trouble?

If your History list does not look like the one in Figure B-5, click the small down arrow to the right of the word "View" at the top of the Explorer bar, then click By Date on the menu.

1. Click the **History button** on the toolbar
   The Explorer bar opens as a pane on the left side of the browser window, as shown in Figure B-5. If other Web sites have been viewed recently with your browser, your list may be considerably longer than the one pictured in this figure. By default, the sites shown for the selected week are arranged by day of the week, and earlier sites visited are listed chronologically by week. The Web pages in each day's list are arranged alphabetically by the name of the site where they are located.

2. If necessary, click **webreference** on the History list to display the name of the page on this site that you have visited
   The "E-Commerce Watch" page you viewed in the second lesson was located on a Web site named "www.webreference.com." All the pages you viewed on this Web site are therefore listed under "webreference" in the History list.

3. Click **E-Commerce Watch** under the webreference heading in the History list
   The electronic commerce page you viewed earlier reopens in the right frame.

4. Click the list arrow to the right of the word "View" at the top of the Explorer bar
   The Explorer bar View menu opens, as shown in Figure B-6. This menu offers different options for organizing the display of history information. The Search option—which appears as both a menu item and a button next to the View menu on the Explorer bar—allows you to replace the History list with a generic form that allows you to search for information on the Web.

5. Click
   The History frame closes, and the E-Commerce Watch page is displayed across the entire browser window.

FIGURE B-5: History window

Explorer bar

History list organized chronologically

Each day's entries organized by Web server

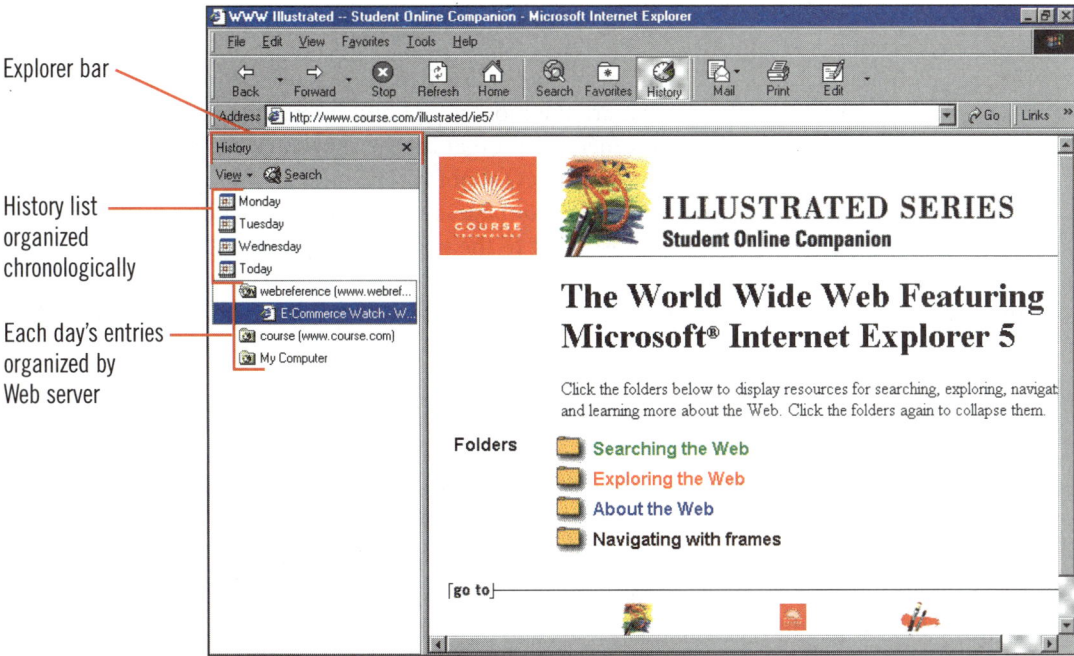

FIGURE B-6: Explorer bar View menu

Click to display Web search form

View options for History list

What is the Explorer bar?

The Explorer bar lets you perform activities, such as navigating using the History list or searching for information on the Web, while the current Web page is displayed on the right side of the browser window. This format allows you to select and view pages from the Explorer bar without closing it. For example, if you click the Search button on the Standard Buttons toolbar, the Explorer bar opens on the left side of the browser window and displays a form for searching on the Web, while continuing to show the site you are currently viewing in the right frame. You can use the form to search for information, and then open one of the suggested Web sites. You can also display your Address bar or Links bar as an Explorer bar in the browser window.

Using Favorites

Internet Explorer provides a convenient feature called Favorites that lets you collect and organize hyperlinks to the Web pages that are the most useful and interesting to you. You can add Web page shortcuts to your Favorites menu and organize the shortcuts into folders by subject. The Favorites menu provides another convenient tool for returning to Web pages that you have already visited. Favorites are especially useful for pages that you find particularly significant and expect to visit repeatedly. As assistant to the marketing manager of The Nut Tree, you think the E-Commerce Watch page will be a useful resource once you are ready to put your company and product information on the Web. Add this page to your Favorites list so you can easily return to it.

Steps

1. **Make sure the E-Commerce Watch page is displayed in your document window, click Favorites on the menu bar, then click Add to Favorites**

   The Add Favorite dialog box opens. The Name text box shows the text that will be used to identify this shortcut on the Favorites list; the page title displayed in the browser's title bar is used as the default. Although you can edit the shortcut name, you decide that the default name is a good description of the page.

> **QuickTip**
>
> To create a shortcut button on the Links toolbar, create a favorite in the Links folder.

2. **If your Add Favorite window does not display the New Folder button, click the Create in button**

   The Add Favorite dialog box expands to include options for placing the new shortcut within a folder on the Favorites menu as shown in Figure B-7. You decide to create a new folder titled "Online marketing" to include this shortcut, as well as links to other pages on this topic that you may come across in the future.

3. **Click the New Folder Button, type Online marketing in the Folder name text box, then click OK**

   The Create New Folder dialog box closes, and you return to the Add Favorite dialog box, with the new folder highlighted on the Favorites list.

4. **Click OK to add this page to your Favorites list with the default name, then click the Home button 🏠 on the toolbar**

   Your home page appears in the document window.

> **QuickTip**
>
> Click the Favorites button on the toolbar to display your Favorites list alphabetically in the Explorer bar.

5. **Click Favorites on the menu bar (not on the Standard Buttons toolbar)**

   The Favorites menu opens, displaying commands for working with the Favorites list as well as the shortcuts themselves, as shown in Figure B-8. Notice that the Channels, Links, Media and Software Updates folders appear beneath these options, in addition to the Online marketing folder that you created.

6. **Point to the Online marketing folder, then click E-CommerceWatch–WebReference.com**

   The Favorites menu closes, and the E-Commerce Watch page opens. If your Favorites list becomes too large, or you find that some shortcuts are no longer valid or useful, you can remove shortcuts and folders.

7. **Click Favorites, click Organize Favorites, click the Online marketing folder, click Delete, then click Yes**

   The shortcut and folder you added are removed from the list.

8. **Click Close in the Organize Favorites dialog box, then click 🏠**

Click to save pages for offline viewing

Name that will identify new shortcut

Your folder list may differ.

Click to create new folder for organizing favorites

Click to choose a location for the new shortcut

FIGURE B-8: Favorites menu

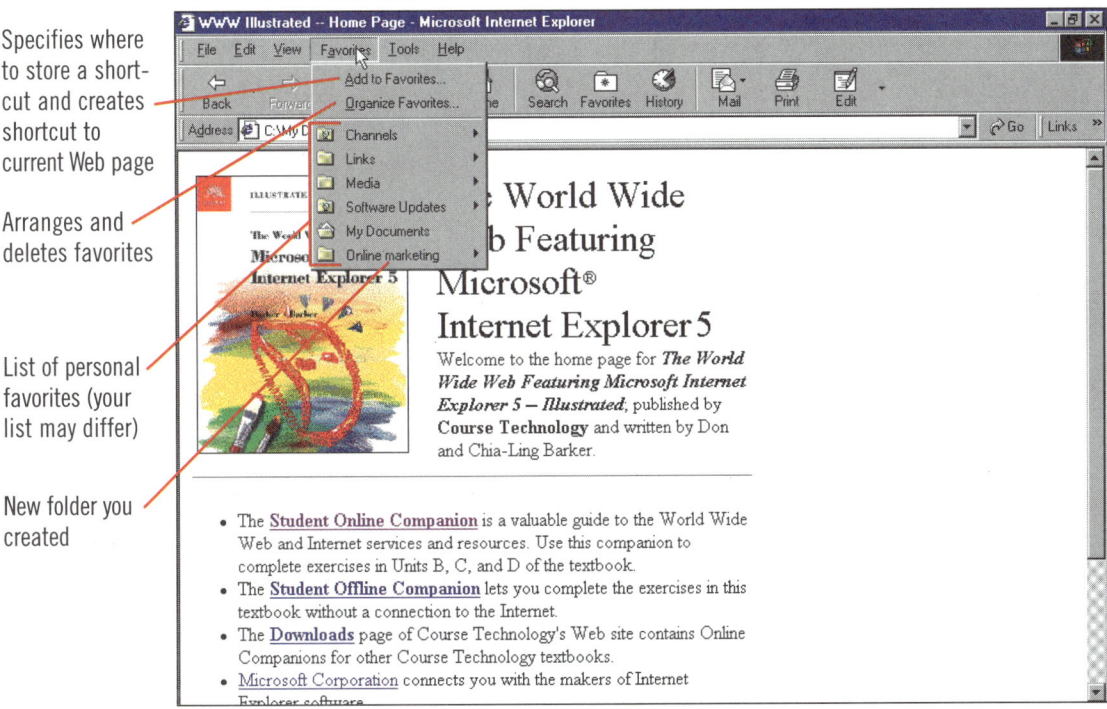

Specifies where to store a short-cut and creates shortcut to current Web page

Arranges and deletes favorites

List of personal favorites (your list may differ)

New folder you created

Viewing Web pages offline

Internet Explorer allows you to view selected pages from your Favorites list even when you are offline, or not connected to the Web. You can mark pages on your Favorites list that you want to view offline. Internet Explorer then saves copies of the Web page files for these marked pages, along with any associated image files, to your computer. You can then view these pages on any browser, whether or not you are connected to the Internet. Viewing pages offline allows you to save pages you haven't thoroughly read, and then view them later when you don't have access to the Web (for example, when using a laptop on an airplane).

To mark a page to be available offline, you select the Make available offline check box in the Add Favorite dialog box. You can also select an existing shortcut in the Organize Favorites dialog box, then click the Make available offline check box. You can use the Customize button in the Add Favorite dialog box, or the Properties button in the Organize Favorites dialog box, to set how often you would like the page updated on your hard drive, and whether you want pages linked on the cur-rent page to be saved as well. After you mark all the pages you want to view offline, click Tools, then click Synchronize to download and save an up-to-date ver-sion of each marked page. Then click File on the menu bar and click Work Offline to let Internet Explorer know that you want to use saved pages, rather than download new versions from the Web.

Internet

Working with Frames

Internet Explorer can divide the document window into smaller windows, called **frames**. Like the Explorer bar, this feature can display new pages in one or more frames, while maintaining the same information in other frames. Frames are a component of Web page design that are added to Web pages by their authors. A common use of frames is to display a set of navigation tools along the top or side of the document window. These tools allow the user to move among a Web site's pages, which are displayed in a different frame, without needing to reload the navigation information for each new Web page. You can use the standard Back and Forward buttons on the Command toolbar to navigate in frames by first clicking an inactive area in the frame whose contents you want to change and then clicking the appropriate button. Table B-2 provides a list of additional right-click commands that are available from within a frame. Frames sound like a useful feature to incorporate into The Nut Tree's Web documents. Familiarize yourself with frames so that you can discuss them with Melissa and make recommendations for their use in the company's Web pages.

1. Click the **Student Online Companion link** or the **Student Offline Companion link** on your home page
   The Student Online Companion page appears in your document window.

2. Click the folder next to the heading **Navigating with frames**, then click the **Student Online Companion using frames link** on the list that appears
   Your document window displays the Student Online Companion in two frames, as shown in Figure B-9. The left frame contains a navigation menu.

3. Click the **Exploring the Web link** in the left frame, then click the **Electronic publishing link** on the list that appears
   The right frame displays the Exploring electronic publishing Web page.

4. To move back one frame on the right, click the right frame, then click the **Back button** ⬅ on the toolbar
   The right frame changes to show the information displayed before you made your selection in the left frame. You can also navigate backward and forward in a frame using the right-click menu.

5. To move forward a frame, right-click the right frame, then click **Forward** on the pop-up menu
   The right frame redisplays the Exploring electronic publishing Web page information.

6. Click the **Home button** 🏠 to return to your home page

QuickTip

If you right-click on an image in a frame instead of in an inactive area, you will receive an entirely different menu of commands than those shown in Table B-2. These commands are designed to work with an image. The same holds true if you right-click on a link in a frame. The menu that appears will contain commands specific for working with hyperlinks.

FIGURE B-9: Student Online Companion formatted with frames

Left frame contains
clickable menu items

Right frame displays results of
menu selections made in left frame

TABLE B-2: Right mouse button commands available when pointing to a frame

command	description
Back	Moves back one page in the frame
Forward	Moves forward one page in the frame
Select All	Highlights all elements of the page in the current frame
Create Shortcut	When double-clicked, creates a desktop icon that automatically displays the page in the frame associated with the current link
Add to Favorites	Adds a shortcut to your Favorites list of the page in the frame
View Source	Displays a window with the code used to create the page in the frame
Encoding	Allows selection of the character set in which the page is displayed (the default, Western European, includes accented characters for French, Spanish, Dutch, etc.; a language like Russian or Chinese would require a different set of characters)
Print	Prints a hard copy of the page in the current frame
Refresh	Reloads the page in the current frame using the latest information from the Web site
Properties	Shows information about the page in the frame

Internet

Customizing the Toolbar

By default, the Internet Explorer 5 toolbar is set up conveniently for most users. However, after becoming familiar with its options and features, and with your own work patterns on the Web, you may find that you would like to change the way the browser appears. Internet Explorer 5 allows you to change the way the Standard toolbar appears by selecting the buttons that appear, and by selecting their format. Now that you have used many of the Standard toolbar buttons, you want to try customizing it to see if other layouts work better for you.

Steps 1 2 3 4

1. Click **View** on the Menu bar, point to **Toolbars**, then click **Customize**
   The Customize Toolbar window opens, as shown in Figure B-10. This window allows you to add or remove buttons from the Standard toolbar, decide if the buttons display with text labels, and choose the size of the toolbar buttons.

QuickTip

The word Separator appears on the icon list wherever a vertical line appears on the Standard toolbar. You can insert a vertical line between any two icons by selecting Separator in the left list box and clicking Add->.

2. Make sure the final list item, **Separator**, is selected in the Current toolbar buttons list, click **Full Screen** in the Available toolbar buttons list, then click Add->.
   The Full Screen button is added to the Current toolbar buttons list, and immediately appears on the Standard toolbar. Table B-3 explains the function of each button in the Available toolbar buttons list.

3. Click the **Text options list arrow**, then click **No text labels**
   The Standard toolbar buttons display much smaller, without associated text.

4. Click **Close**
   Figure B-11 shows the new appearance of the Standard toolbar. Because the buttons are shorter, more of your home page is visible in the document window.

5. Click **View** on the Menu bar, point to **Toolbars**, click **Customize**, then click **Reset**
   Because you are not using your own computer, you change the settings back to their defaults. Full Screen is removed from the Current toolbar buttons list, and the appearance of the Standard toolbar changes to reflect the default settings.

6. Click **Close**

FIGURE B-10: Links toolbar

Lists buttons not currently part of toolbar

Returns all toolbar settings to defaults

Lists current toolbar buttons

Positions selected button further left on the toolbar

Positions selected button further right on the toolbar

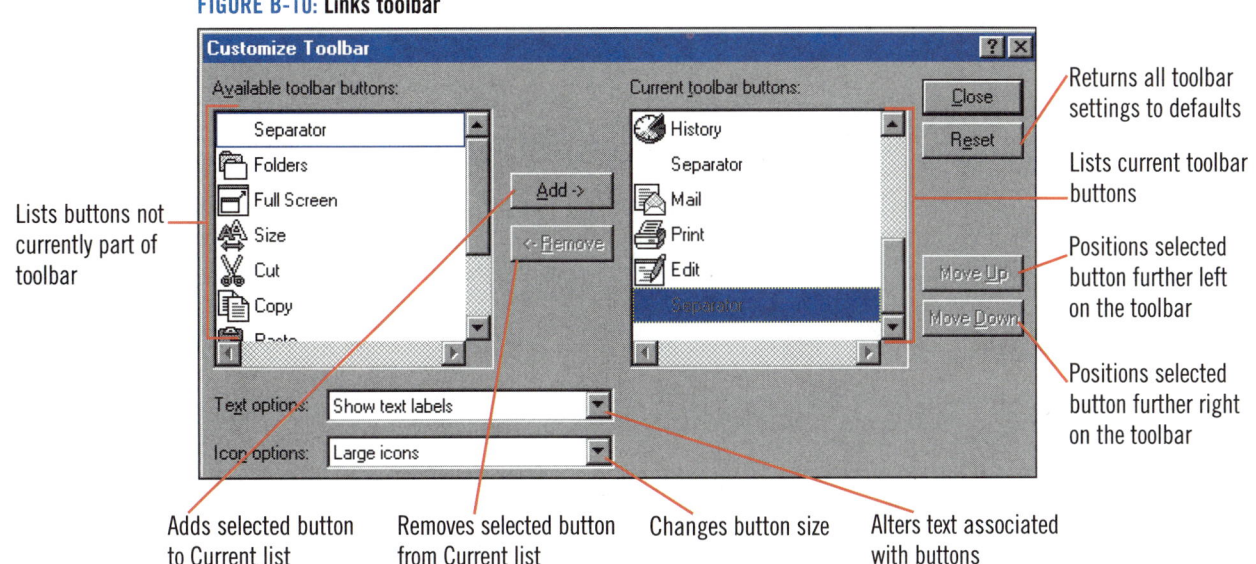

Adds selected button to Current list

Removes selected button from Current list

Changes button size

Alters text associated with buttons

FIGURE B-11: Web Directory page

Toolbar buttons appear without text labels

Expanded document window shows more of Web page

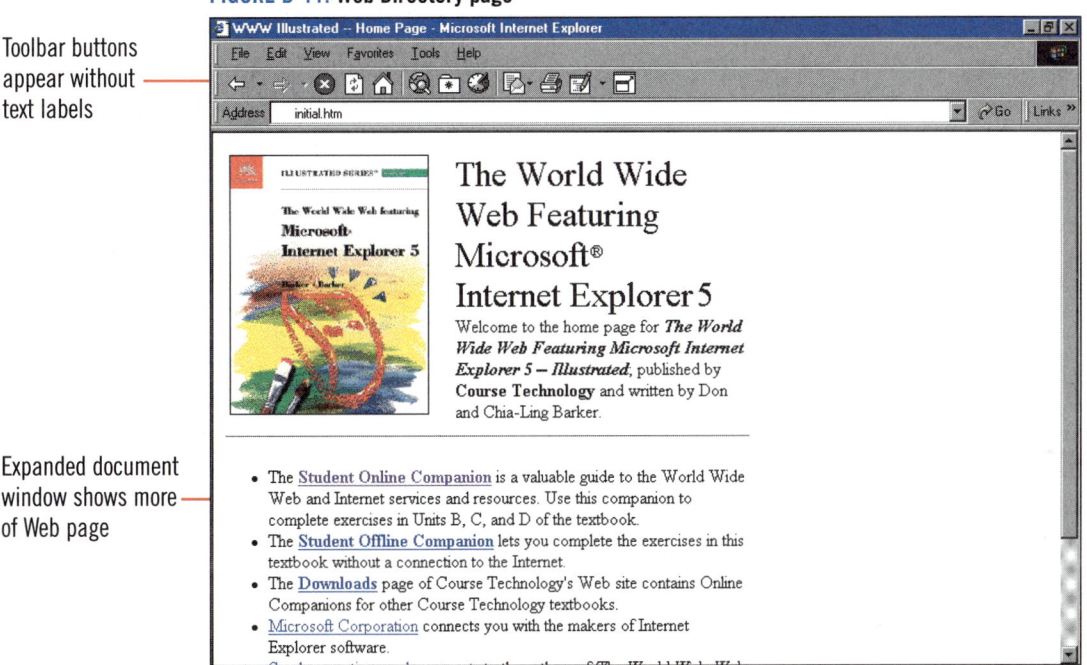

TABLE B-3: Available toolbar buttons

button	description
	Opens a list of local and network directories in the Explorer bar
	Displays current Web page with only a narrow toolbar, devoting more screen space to the page
	Increases or decreases the font size for text in the document window
	Removes selected element from the document window, placing it on the Windows clipboard
	Places a copy of the selected element in the document window on the Windows clipboard
	Replaces the selected element in the document window with the contents of the Windows clipboard
	Allows you to select what alphabet Internet Explorer uses for the text in documents you open
	Lists other Web pages related to the page in the document window

Internet

Entering a URL

Hyperlinks make navigating the Web as simple as pointing and clicking. Sometimes you want to view a Web page you have heard about, but don't have a link to the page. In this case, you need to type the page's address, which is its URL. You enter a URL in the Address text box on the Address bar in Internet Explorer. You found a list of Web sites for popular specialty food items in a magazine and made a list of the company names and URLs (shown in Table B-3) to provide ideas for The Nut Tree's home page. Enter the URL for Somis Nut House to view the firm's Web page.

Steps 1234

1. **Click the Address text box on the Address bar**
   The current URL becomes highlighted in the Address text box.

QuickTip

If you are using the Student Offline Companion, the "C|/Offline/" in the address represents one possible disk drive and folder location for the Offline Companion files. Your instructor or technical support person may provide you with an alternate drive and folder to use in completing these steps.

2. **Type www.somisnuthouse.com/ in the Address text box; or, if you are using the Student Offline Companion, type file:///C|/Offline/somisnuthouse/index.htm**
   The old URL and page icon disappear as you type the new URL, as shown in Figure B-12. Note that the "|" in the offline file address is the pipe symbol (press [Shift] [\]).

3. **Press [Enter]**
   If you are working online, Internet Explorer automatically adds http:// at the beginning of the address you typed. The status indicator becomes animated, and the Somis Nut House Web page appears shortly, as pictured in Figure B-13. (If you receive an error message while trying to open the Somis Nut House page, enter another URL listed in Table B-3.)

4. **Explore the page, then click the Address text box on the Address bar**
   The text box still displays the URL you entered earlier. You can use your edit keys to modify this address rather than typing in an entirely new URL.

QuickTip

To save time in typing in a new URL, type in just the middle part of the URL (for example, "microsoft") and then press [Ctrl][Enter]; "http://www" is automatically added to the front of the address and ".com" to the end.

5. **Click at the end of the previous URL address in the Address text box**
   A flashing insertion point (text cursor) appears at the end of the URL.

6. **Press [Backspace] as many times as necessary to erase everything after http://www. or, if you are using the Student Offline Companion, after the local pathname (e.g., file:///C|/Offline/)**
   The Address text box now displays only the beginning of a URL address, http://www., or a local pathname.

7. **Type godiva.com and press [Enter] or, if you are using the Student Offline Companion, type godiva/index.htm and press [Enter]**
   The status indicator becomes animated again and, after a brief time, the document window displays the initial page at the Godiva Chocolatier company's Web site.

8. **Click the Home button ⌂ on the toolbar**
   The document window displays your home page.

9. **Exit Internet Explorer**

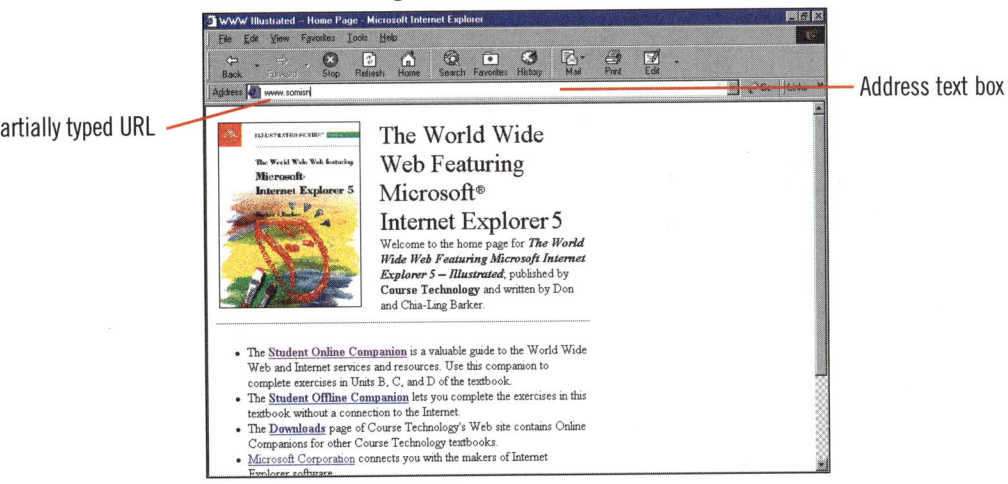

Partially typed URL

Address text box

FIGURE B-13: Home page for Somis Nut House

TABLE B-4: URLs of potential competitors for The Nut Tree

company name	URL
Somis Nut House	http://www.somisnuthouse.com/
Long Grove Confectionery Company	http://www.longgrove.com/
Ann Hemyng Candy Inc.'s Chocolate Factory	http://mmink.com/mmink/dossiers/choco.html
North Dakota 24K Karamels	http://www.petergreywolf.com/caramels.htm
Rowena's	http://www.pilotonline.com/rowenas/

CLUES TO USE

AutoComplete

When you are manually entering a URL, the AutoComplete feature fills in the remaining portion of URLs you've recently typed, based on the first few letters you type in the Address bar. Additionally, when you type the beginning characters for a site where you have visited multiple pages, Internet Explorer opens a drop-down menu displaying the URLs of all the pages you opened previously. If the page you want to open is listed, you can simply click it on the list to open it, rather then typing the remainder of the address.

Practice

► Concepts Review

Label the elements of the Web address and the Location toolbar shown in Figure B-14.

FIGURE B-14

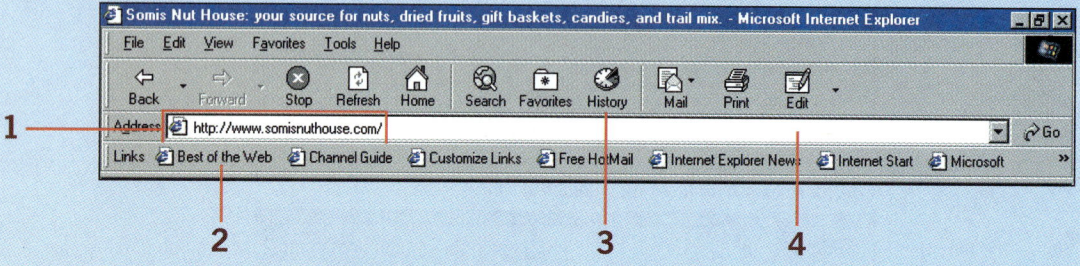

Match each of the terms below with the statement that best describes its function.

5. Add to Favorites
6. Forward button
7. URL
8. Home button
9. Back button
10. History button

a. Returns you to your home page
b. Loads the previously viewed page
c. Creates a shortcut to a Web page
d. Jumps to the next page in a series of previously viewed pages
e. Address of a Web page
f. Displays recently visited Web pages

Select the best answer from the list of choices.

11. A hyperlink in a Web page lets you
   a. Jump to another Web page.
   b. Connect two hyper-zones.
   c. Load a paper page.
   d. Create fail-safe linkages.

12. To view the previous page
   a. Click the Previous button.
   b. Click the Back button.
   c. Click the Previous command on the Go menu.
   d. Select the Backup command on the Go menu.

13. The Favorites menu lets you do everything *except*
   a. Add the current page to the Favorites list.
   b. Store a shortcut to the current page in a folder.
   c. Open the Organize Favorites window.
   d. Move a page around the Web.

14. **The History Explorer bar lets you do everything** *except*
    a. View the History list by page title.
    b. Search for a particular previously viewed page.
    c. Create a hyperlink.
    d. View a previously visited page.

15. **Which URL is incorrect?**
    a. http://www.company.com
    b. http://www.company.com/home.html
    c. http://www.company/home.html
    d. http://www.company.com/homepage.html

16. **HTTP stands for**
    a. Hypertext Translate Protocol.
    b. Hypertext Transfer Pilot.
    c. Hypertext Transfer Protocol.
    d. Hypertext Transport Pointer.

17. **The _____ usually follows "www." in a Web site's name, and tells you both the name of the Web site and the type of institution it is.**
    a. Top-level domain
    b. Domain name
    c. Origin name
    d. URL

18. **The global domain .org means the Web site you are accessing is a**
    a. Commercial site.
    b. Nonprofit organization site.
    c. Military site.
    d. Educational site.

19. **A link you have previously followed appears on the screen (by default) in**
    a. Red.
    b. Green.
    c. Purple.
    d. Blue.

20. **The newest items added to your favorites will initially appear**
    a. At the top.
    b. At the bottom.
    c. Alphabetically.
    d. Under the heading New Entries at the end of the existing bookmark.

▶ Skills Review

1. **Find, start, and stop hyperlinks.**
   a. Start Internet Explorer.
   b. Click the Student Online Companion link or the Student Offline Companion link on your home page.
   c. Click the Exploring the Web folder, then click the Exploring electronic commerce folder.
   d. Click one of the links in the list that appears, then click the Stop button on the toolbar before the page finishes loading.
   e. Click the Refresh button to finish loading the page.

2. **Move backward and forward.**
   a. Click the Back button to return to the Student Online Companion page.
   b. Click the Forward button to see the electronic commerce page you opened.
   c. Continue to click the Back button until it dims.
   d. Click the Forward button to display the next page.
   e. Choose a link from one of the folders. Once the new page loads, use the Back and Forward buttons to locate the Student Online Companion page.

3. **View History.**
   a. Click the History button on the toolbar.
   b. Click WWW Illustrated–Student Online Companion in the list under the www.course.com folder.
   c. Click the Home button.
   d. Use the Back button list arrow to return to the page you just viewed.
   e. Close the Explorer bar.

4. **Use Favorites.**
   a. Click the Home button on the toolbar.
   b. Click the Add to Favorites command on the Favorites menu, if necessary click Create in, click New Folder, type "Internet Explorer," click OK, type "Internet Explorer", then click OK twice.
   c. Load the Student Online Companion or Student Offline Companion page.
   d. Add the current page to your Favorites list in the Internet Explorer folder.
   e. Click the Explore the Web folder, click the Exploring electronic publishing folder, then click one of the links on the list that appears.
   f. Use the Favorites menu to return to the WWW Illustrated–Student Online Companion page.
   g. If you're working in a computer lab, remove the Favorites shortcuts you added.

5. Work with frames.

  a. Click the Home button on the toolbar.

  b. Click the <u>Student Online Companion</u> or <u>Student Offline Companion</u> link.

  c. Click the Navigating with frames folder, then click the <u>Student Online Companion using frames</u> link.

  d. Click the <u>Exploring the Web</u> link in the left frame menu, then click the <u>Electronic commerce</u> link.

  e. Move back one page in the right frame.

  f. Click another link on the navigation menu in the left frame, then move back one page again in the right frame, using the right-click menu.

  g. Click the Home button on the toolbar to display your home page.

6. Customize the toolbar.

  a. Click View on the Menu bar, point to Toolbars, then click Customize.

  b. Make sure the final list item, Separator, is selected in the Current toolbar buttons list, click copy in the Available toolbar buttons list, then click Add->.

  c. Click the Icon options list arrow, then click Small icons.

  d. Click Close.

  e. Click View on the Menu bar, point to Toolbars, click Customize, then click Reset.

  f. Click Close.

7. Enter a URL address.

  a. Click the Address text box on the Address bar.

  b. In the Location text box, type "www.ibm.com" or, if you're using the Student Offline Companion, type "file:///c|/offline/ibm/index.htm".

  c. Press Enter.

  d. Explore this Web site, using the techniques and tools you learned about in this unit.

  e. Click the Home button on the toolbar when you have finished, then exit Internet Explorer.

Independent Challenges

1. You are the administrative assistant to John Prescott, the president of Words and Wisdom, a small promotional company that specializes in writing ads, promotional pieces, and jingles. John travels a great deal while promoting his company's services. He wants to trade his desktop computer for a notebook computer that he can carry on his business trips. John has narrowed the search down to five computer makers, and he asks you to investigate their offerings using the Web. The computer firms' URLs are as follows:

www.compaq.com
www.ibm.com
www.apple.com
www.hp.com
www.nec-computers.com

Use Internet Explorer to research the information available on the Web for each firm's notebooks, then print a page from the site of the firm you think offers the most attractive notebook computer line.

2. You recently landed a job as a columnist for a popular computer magazine. One of your responsibilities will be to write a monthly column called Tech Update, which will chronicle the latest developments in hardware technology. Add the following Web sites to a new folder on your Favorites list so you can browse them for information that will help you stay abreast of the activities of the major players in the computer hardware industry:

www.compaq.com
www.dell.com
www.apple.com
www.hp.com

Once you store the initial pages of these sites in the Favorites list, use the list to revisit the initial page for each site and investigate the company's offerings. Print a page of the site that most impresses you, and then remove the folder containing the shortcuts from the Favorites list.

3. In a few months, you will graduate from college with a teaching degree. You have been investigating the job market, but you are also interested in traveling and perhaps teaching in a different country. A friend suggests that you consider the Peace Corps, and you decide to look into the organization. Use the following URL to research the Peace Corps: www.peacecorps.gov
Explore the site, then print a page containing useful information.

4. You are teaching a course on the United States government. You're preparing to assign a research project to your students to discuss and compare the three branches of the U.S. government—executive (the president, cabinet, and administrative departments), legislative (Congress), and judicial (the courts). You want to require your students to do some of their research on the Internet. You investigate a list of URLs for government sites given to you by a colleague, to make sure this is a reasonable expectation. To complete this Independent Challenge, open and investigate the offerings on the following Web sites. Keep written notes on each site, recording the types of information available and the approximate number of Web pages for each. After you have surveyed each site, write a paragraph discussing whether or not you think the Internet is a reasonable source of information for this project.
www.whitehouse.gov
www.house.gov
www.senate.gov
www.uscourts.gov

Visual Workshop

Use the skills you learned in this lesson to open the Web page below, then navigate as necessary to activate both the Back and Forward buttons, as shown in Figure B-15. Print a copy of the page.

FIGURE B-15

Searching
the Web

The World Wide Web is an enormous network, and when you want to find information on a particular subject, simply navigating from one page to the next is a very slow and inefficient way to go about it. Fortunately, a number of search tools available on the Web can help you quickly locate what you want. Using these tools, you can find information on a certain topic, resources in a certain geographical location, or simply an acquaintance's address information. Before you begin developing an online marketing effort for The Nut Tree Company, you want to understand better how people find information on the Web using search tools, and therefore how they might seek out information about The Nut Tree Company. In addition, it will be helpful to understand these resources in order to use them yourself in gathering information day-to-day in your job. In this unit, you will learn how to use these search tools effectively and efficiently to locate information.

Understanding Search Methods

Information on the Web grows rapidly, is not well organized, and sometimes proves inaccurate. As a consequence, it is important to search as effectively and efficiently as possible. Some search tools are better for finding a specific type of information than others. Typically, an integrated approach that combines the available search tools gives you the best chance of finding the information you want. Table C-1 indicates strategies for finding information with each of the major search tools that will be discussed in this unit. ✎▬▬ To use your time most effectively when doing Web research for The Nut Tree Company, use the following integrated strategies, or guidelines, to minimize your search time and maximize search results.

Details

 Search broadly at first to determine the breadth of information available on the subject.

 Search narrowly and deeply to find specific information.

 Search multiple sources simultaneously to ensure greater coverage of the Web.

 Look for pages with collections of links about a subject.

 Look for interlinked pages related to a subject.

 Locate sites related to a subject.

 Locate people, using "white page" sites.

TABLE C-1: Strategies for searching the Web

to find	example information	search by	tool	example tools
General categories of information	Electronic commerce	Subject	**Subject directories** are hand-compiled lists of sites grouped and arranged by topic.	Yahoo! and Galaxy
Narrow and specific information	Buying nuts	Content	**Search engines** automatically scan the Web and index it by keyword.	AltaVista and Excite
Extensive resources for narrow and specific information	Buying nuts	Content	**Metasearch engines** offer single forms for querying multiple search engines' indices simultaneously.	Dogpile and Metacrawler
Pages with collections of links about a subject	Information about search engines	Collection	**Collections** are guide pages with useful information about a subject.	Search Engine Watch and Browser Watch
Related pages linked together in a circle	Shopping online	Webring	**RingWorld** is the "hub" of related pages linked together to form easily navigated rings.	RingWorld
Regional Web site	Food or gift shops online in Spokane, WA	Location	**Location maps and directories** are graphics and lists that organize Web sites geographically.	OnLineNow and W3 Servers
A person's e-mail or Web site address	A lost business contact	People	**People finders** are searchable indices for locating people.	Switchboard and 411 Locate

CLUES TO USE

Additional Search Tools

Microsoft Internet Explorer 5 offers several features to help with searches, such as AutoSearch, Related Links, and the Windows Radio Toolbar. AutoSearch lets you type a search query directly into the Address bar of your browser and uses Microsoft's search engine to locate possible matches on the Web. Related Links is an optional feature that provides you with a list of sites similar to the one you are currently viewing in your browser. The Windows Radio Toolbar helps you find radio stations you can listen to over the Web. For details about these search features, visit Microsoft's Web site at http://www.microsoft.com/windows/ie.

Internet

Searching by Subject

If you are not sure where to start investigating a subject, or if you want to obtain a quick overview of a subject, begin your search with a subject directory. A **subject directory** is a list of links to general information topics, arranged alphabetically to facilitate browsing. Experts usually compile subject directories, making them a fairly reliable search tool. These hand-compiled directories typically list subtopics beneath each major heading, as shown in Figure C-1. The hierarchical organization, or hierarchical tree, in a subject directory lets you quickly browse through the available subjects and their subtopics. Melissa Shea, marketing manager for The Nut Tree, asks you to research the commercial services available on the Web as part of the plan to establish an online presence for the company. You can use Yahoo! to determine what types of business services are available via the Web.

Steps 1 2 3 4

1. **Open your browser, then click the <u>Student Online Companion</u> link on your home page or, if you are working offline, click the <u>Student Offline Companion</u> link**
   The Student Online Companion for this textbook appears in your document window.

2. **Click the Searching the Web folder, then click the Searching by subject folder**
   A list of links to subject directories appears in your document window below the Searching by subject folder.

Trouble?

If you are unable to connect to Yahoo! (for example, if you receive an error message or the page fails to load after a long time), select another subject directory from the Searching by subject page and explore its structure to complete this lesson.

3. **Click <u>Yahoo!</u>**
   The Yahoo! page opens, as shown in Figure C-2. The top of the page features a Search box to assist in locating a subject (you will learn about search boxes and forms in the "Searching by Content" lesson). For now, you will browse the subject directory just below the Search box to gain an overview of the business resources available on the Web.

4. **Click <u>Business and Economy</u> in the subject directory, then scroll down the page that loads to view the options available on the subject list**
   A list of topics having to do with business and economy appears, as shown in Figure C-3.

5. **Click <u>Electronic Commerce</u>**
   A directory of electronic commerce topics appears.

6. **Scroll down the list and examine the available topics**

7. **When you have finished, return to your home page**

FIGURE C-1: Alphabetical and hierarchical structure of a subject directory

Major subject heading

Subtopic

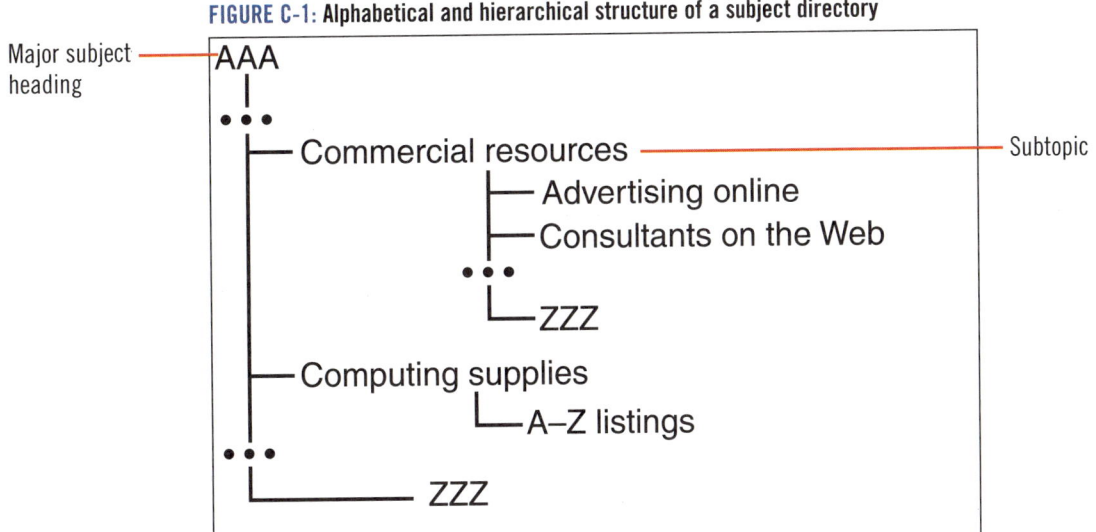

FIGURE C-2: Yahoo! home page

Business & Economy link

FIGURE C-3: Listing of Business and Economy subtopics on Yahoo!

Electronic Commerce link

Internet

Internet

Searching by Content

When you want to find specific information, your best option is a search engine. A **search engine** lets you specify key words or phrases so as to retrieve a list of links to pages on the Web that contain matching information. A search engine uses a special program called a "spider" to travel from one Web site to another, indexing the contents of the Web pages at each site. The **index** created by the spider is simply a list of the keywords with links to the pages they appear on. To search an index, you carefully craft a query, using key words and phrases, and enter it in a search form provided by the search engine. A more precisely worded query will yield more relevant results. ✎ Impressed by the electronic commerce content that you have discovered, you decide to search for information about buying nuts on the Web. Because you have a specific topic in mind, "buying nuts," the most expedient way to conduct the search is via a search engine.

1. Click the <u>Student Online Companion</u> link or the <u>Student Offline Companion</u> link on your home page, click the **Searching the Web folder**, then click the **Searching by content folder**

A list of links to search engines on the Web appears below the Searching by content folder.

QuickTip

If AltaVista is busy, click the link for another search engine instead.

2. Click <u>AltaVista</u>

The simple search form for the AltaVista search engine opens, as shown in Figure C-4. All search engines provide you with two basic elements to use to search. The **Search text box** is where you enter the word or words for which you want to search. The **Search button** is the button that you click in order to start the search once you have entered information in the Search text box. See Table C-2 for a description of the additional options provided by AltaVista.

QuickTip

Many search engines now provide subject directories to help narrow the topics to search on the Web. However, these directories are typically generated automatically and, thus, lack the same relevance as hand-compiled directories such as Yahoo!

3. Click in the **Search text box** to make the insertion point appear, then type **"buying nuts"**

The search statement must contain double quotes (" ") at the end and beginning. This format tells the AltaVista search engine to look only for pages that contain all of your key words together and in the precise order in which you have entered them (i.e., when they appear as a phrase). The ability to search for an exact phrase narrows your search results significantly. If you don't add quotes or otherwise indicate that you are searching for an exact phrase, the search engine will match every page indexed that contains any, or all, of the key words, regardless of where they appear in the pages. This makes the search much less useful for finding relevant information.

4. Click the **Search button**

The search page reloads, showing the results of the query.

QuickTip

Search results may also contain other useful hints, such as relevancy scores. These scores rate and arrange retrieved Web pages according to how closely they match your query. Relevancy scoring typically uses the proximity of key words (that is, how close the words are to one another) in a page and their frequency in a page to rank the results of a search.

5. Scroll down the page to see the results

The results appear below the search form, beginning with a summary statement that specifies the number of pages matching your query, as shown in Figure C-5. AltaVista displays the results sorted according to how closely they match your query. If a query is poorly constructed, the matches, or hits, can number in the hundreds of thousands, making it nearly impossible to look at all of them.

6. Click the first, most relevant link

A page appears in your document window.

7. Examine the page, then return to the results page

8. Scroll to the bottom of the page, then click <u>next>></u>

The page containing the next set of links leading to matching pages appears.

9. When you have finished, return to your home page

FIGURE C-4: AltaVista search form

Search form

Specialty Searches

Search categories

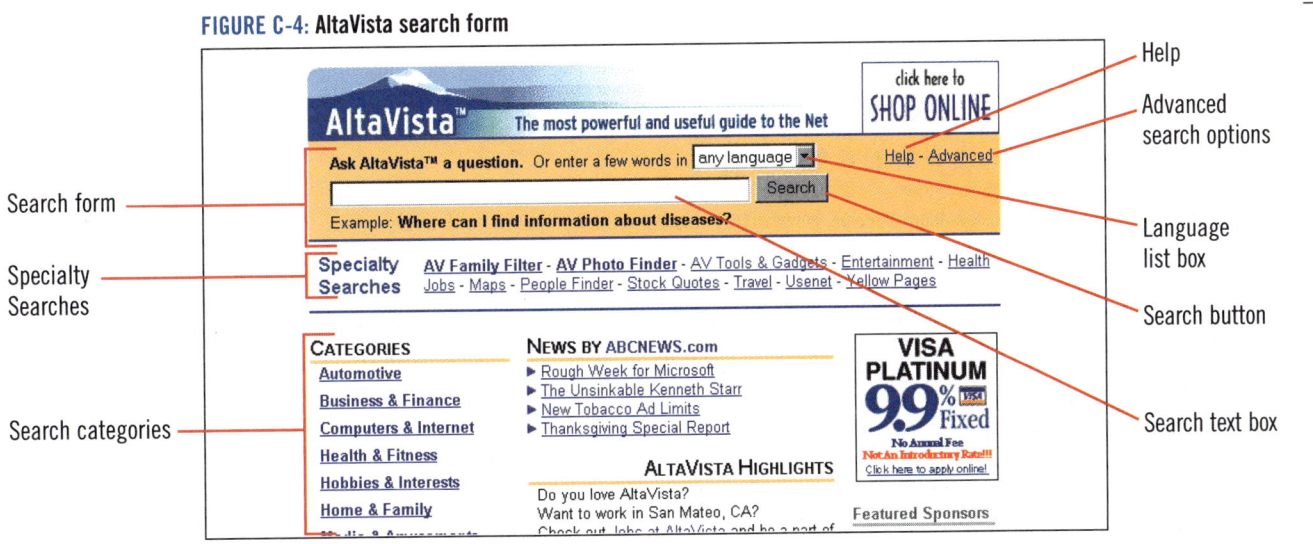

Help

Advanced search options

Language list box

Search button

Search text box

FIGURE C-5: AltaVista search results

Total number of Web pages found by search

Links to matching documents

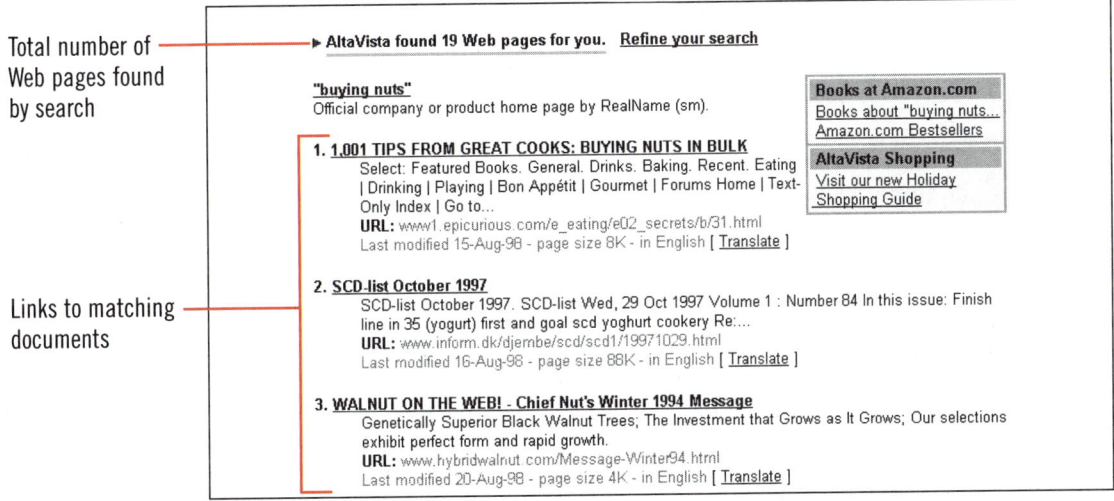

TABLE C-2: Additional options in the AltaVista search form

option	description
Help link	Provides useful search tips on using the simple and advanced search forms to obtain the most relevant results
Language list box	Specifies the language to search in
Advanced link	Switches to a search form with more detailed querying features (e.g., allows Boolean expressions)

Constructing successful queries

The way to find the most relevant results from a search engine is to construct your query using Boolean operators. **Boolean operators** are special connecting words that indicate the relationship among the key words in your search statement. The Boolean operators AND, OR, and NOT let you narrow, broaden, or exclude information retrieved in a search, respectively. Search engines vary in their level and support of Boolean operators, so you should read the help section of the particular search engine you are working with for tips on using the available Boolean search operators.

Internet

Metasearching by Content

A **metasearch tool**, or **engine**, offers a single form to search a variety of powerful search engine indices simultaneously, based on key words or phrases. These unified search interfaces provide a very powerful, convenient, and quick way to cover a lot of ground. They also require more Internet resources (i.e., bandwidth and Web server capacity) and should, therefore, be used judiciously to ensure that resources remain available to other Internet users. ✒ To ensure that you have seen a comprehensive list of information about buying nuts on the Web, you decide to try using a metasearch engine to check the major search engine indices simultaneously for other possible listings.

Steps 1 2 3 4

1. Click the <u>**Student Online Companion**</u> **link** or the <u>**Student Offline Companion**</u> **link** on your home page, click the **Searching the Web folder**, then click the **Metasearching by content folder**

2. Click <u>**Dogpile**</u>
   The search form for Dogpile opens, as shown in Figure C-6. Notice that the search form for Dogpile contains a Search text box, and that there is a Fetch button to click to initiate the search. Table C-3 describes the additional options available in this particular search form.

3. Click the **Search text box**, then type **"buying nuts"**

4. Click the **Fetch button**
   When the search is completed, Dogpile displays a listing of results collated by search engine, along with the total number of matches found.

5. Scroll down the page to view the results
   The collated results for GoTo.com appear, as shown in Figure C-7.

6. Explore another link or two, then return to your home page

Trouble?

AltaVista may return a different number of matches using Dogpile than it did when directly queried in the earlier lesson. Individual search engines often offer unique querying configurations and capabilities that are unavailable when using a metasearch site. To maximize your results, you should use individual search engines in conjunction with metasearch engines.

FIGURE C-6: Dogpile search form

Search for text box →

Fetch (search) button →

Search in radio buttons

FIGURE C-7: Dogpile's collated results from query

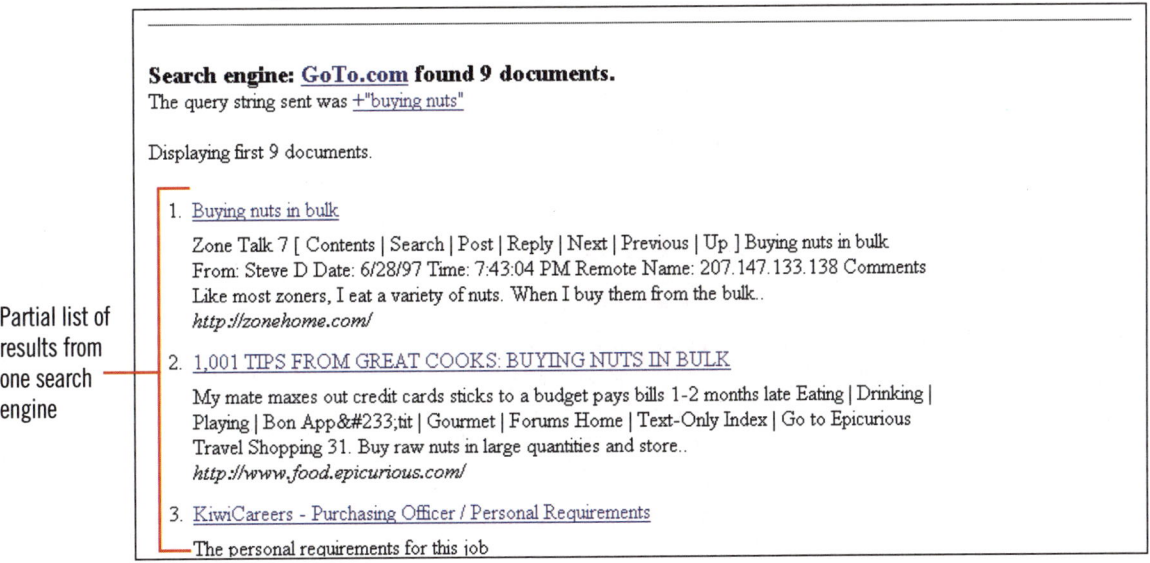

Partial list of results from one search engine

TABLE C-3: Options in the Dogpile search form

option	description
Search for text box	Allows entry of a search query
Fetch button	Starts the search process, which returns a list of results
Search radio button	Indicates specific areas or categories to search on the Internet

Internet

Internet

Searching by Collection

Hundreds of thousands of Web sites already exist, and the number of sites continues to double nearly every two months. To help Web users find useful information about a topic, individuals and organizations that are interested in or dedicated to a particular subject create **collections**, or guides, which offer information and links to Web sites related to that subject. Some collections provide helpful overviews of the subject, in-depth articles, and insightful pointers to further resources. ✒️━━ Intrigued by what you have found so far, you want to find out more about how search engines work.

Steps 1 2 3 4

1. Click the **Student Online Companion link** or the **Student Offline Companion link** on your home page, click the **Searching the Web folder**, then click the **Searching by collection folder**

2. Click **Search Engine Watch**
   A page with news, tips, and more about search engines appears, as shown in Figure C-8.

3. Click one of the links to another page about search engines (e.g., **Search Engines Facts and Fun**)

4. A page like the one shown in Figure C-9 appears. Scroll down the page, then click a link (e.g., **Search Engine Glossary**)
   Figure C-10 shows a partial list of glossary terms for search engines.

5. Go back and explore some of the other links that interest you

6. When you have finished, return to your home page
   Your home page reappears in the document window.

FIGURE C-8: Search Engine Watch: News, Tips and More About Search Engines

FIGURE C-9: Search Engines Facts and Fun

FIGURE C-10: Search Engine Glossary

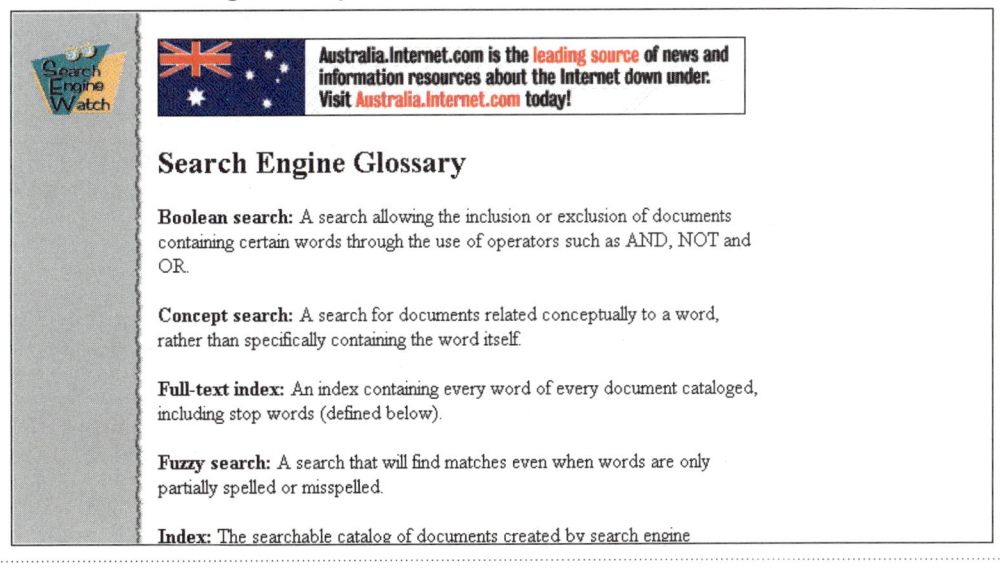

Internet

Searching by Webring

A **Webring** is a group of Web pages related to a topic and linked together to form a ring, or circle. Each page in a Webring is connected by a forward and backward link, so if you follow a ring long enough you will eventually arrive back where you started. **RingWorld** is the subject directory, or "hub," where you search or browse for a Webring about a particular topic. A Webring may have anywhere from five to thousands of pages. Webrings are useful for finding related information in an easy-to-navigate format. You have heard that Webrings offer highly specialized and valuable resources on a variety of subjects, so you decide to see what they offer in the way of information about retail shopping online that might be valuable for creating a Web presence for The Nut Tree Company.

1. Click the **Student Online Companion link** or the **Student Offline Companion link** on your home page, click the **Searching the Web folder**, then click the **Searching by Webring folder**

2. Click **Webring**
   The WebRing home page appears, as shown in Figure C-11.

3. Scroll down the page to view **RingWorld, the WebRing Directory**
   Table C-4 briefly describes the main subject categories and subcategories listed in RingWorld, the WebRing Directory.

Trouble?

If the links in this or subsequent steps have changed, look for other links to business resources on the page.

4. Click **Business and Economy**
   A page with business and economy subcategories loads, as shown in Figure C-12.

5. Click **Products and Services**, scroll down the list of Webrings that appears, then click one about shopping
   A listing of pages in the Webring loads.

6. Click an interesting Web page from the list
   A page from the selected Webring loads. Each page in a Webring has a set of navigation links or buttons. Although Webring pages vary in the number and appearance of navigation controls, they typically contain links to select the Next and Previous pages in the ring. Some pages also feature options that let you view a summary of the next five pages in the Webring or choose a random page from the ring. Webring navigational controls often appear toward the bottom of the page.

7. Find and click the **Next link** to move forward one page in the ring
   The next page in the Webring appears in the browser.

8. Examine the information on the page, and then move forward one page in the ring by clicking the **Next link** again
   You advance to the next page in the Webring.

9. Find and click the **Previous link** to go back one page in the ring, then click the **Random link** to load a random page in the Webring

10. When you have finished, return to your home page

FIGURE C-11: WebRing includes a searchable directory of Webrings called RingWorld

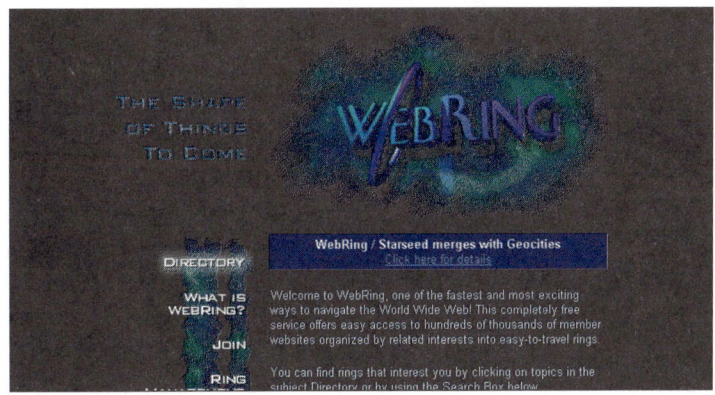

FIGURE C-12: RingWorld Business and Economy index page

Most Popular Rings link

Subcategories

Products and Services

Number of rings in category

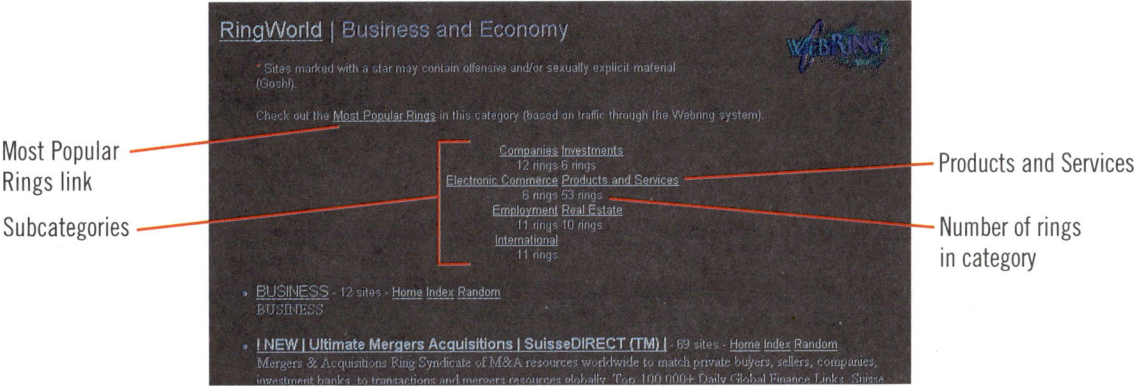

TABLE C-4: Webring subject categories

category	description	example subcategories
Arts and Humanities	Webrings about art, graphics, literature, music, and the theater	Artists, Children, Countries and Cultures, Music, Museums and Galleries, and Theater
Business and Economy	Webrings about companies, e-commerce, employment, investments, and products and services	Companies, Electronic Commerce, Employment, International, Investments, Products and Services, and Real Estate
Computers	Webrings about networking, software, and hardware	Games, Graphics, Hardware, Programming Software, and Windows
Internet	Webrings concerned with the World Wide Web and other Net services	World Wide Web, Miscellaneous Homepages, and Organizations
Health	Webrings about disease, medicine, and health publications	Disease, Education, Medicine, Organizations, and Publications
Recreation and Sports	Webrings about automobiles, airplanes, games, hobbies and crafts, sports, and travel	Automotive, Aviation, Games, Hobbies and Crafts, Outdoors, Sports, Travel, Water Sports
Entertainment	Webrings that feature Japanese anime, comics, humor, movies, people, science fiction, and TV	Anime, Comics and Animation, Cartoons, Humor, Movies, Music, People, Science Fiction, and TV
Society and Culture	Webrings that cover such areas as civil rights, cyberculture, and philosophy	Charity, Civil Rights, Cyberculture, Environment and Nature, Organizations, Religion, and Philosophy
Miscellaneous	Webrings that cover topics that don't fit into the other categories	Animals and Pets, International, News and Current Events, Reference, Regional, Science, and Social Science

Internet

Searching by Location

Location directories and maps are an excellent way to find Web sites in a certain geographical region. A location directory or map lets you specify a region (e.g., city, state, or country) in which to look for information and displays the Web sites available in that geographic area. For example, if you wanted to find the Web sites in your city, you would simply select your city name from a search form in a location directory, then browse the list of sites the service finds. You would like to see what kinds of local businesses and services are available on the Web. The Nut Tree is located in Seattle, WA. You can use Web maps to find a collection of sites to call or visit personally.

Steps 1234

1. Click the **Student Online Companion** link or the **Student Offline Companion** link on your home page, click the **Searching the Web folder**, then click the **Searching by location folder**

2. Click **OnLineNow**
   The OnLineNow page appears with options to search by U.S. city, international city, and by country, as shown in Figure C-13.

3. Click the list arrow on the right of the Select U.S. City list box, scroll down, then click **Seattle-WA**

4. Click the **Go icon** just to the right of the list box
   After some time, a page loads with a list of business links for Seattle, as shown in Figure C-14.

5. Scroll down the page until you find a site offering health food or gifts, then click it
   A separate browser window opens with the home page for the site, like the one shown in Figure C-15.

6. When you have finished, return to your home page

FIGURE C-13: OnLineNow search form

Search U.S. City
list arrow

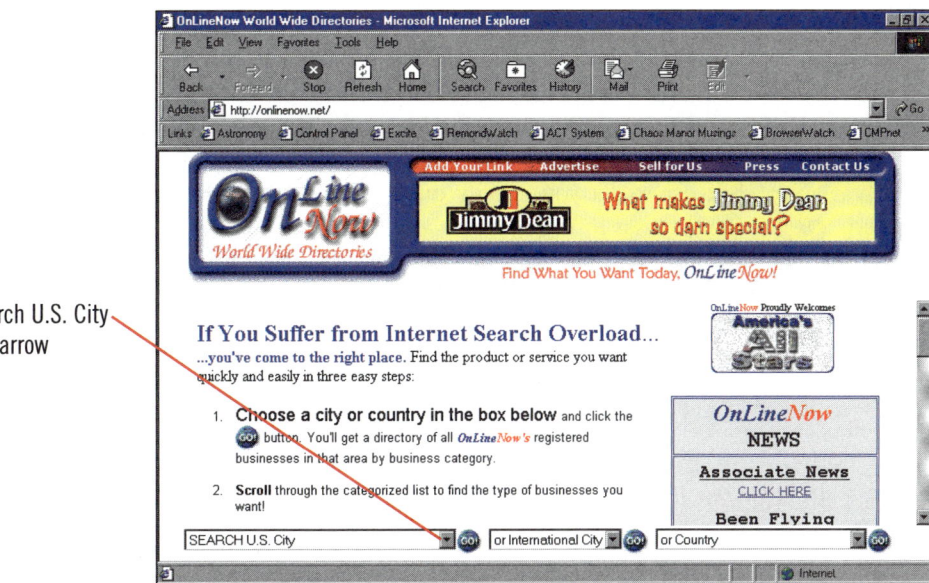

FIGURE C-14: Directory of business Web sites in Seattle, WA

Number of links
found

FIGURE C-15: Example shopping Web site in Seattle

Unit C

Internet

Searching by Person

A people search site assists you in locating some of the 30 million to 60 million people on the Internet. You can search for a person's e-mail address, Web page, and other contact information by name and other variables. Most people directories rely on the individual's name as the key search variable, while others let you specify query topics such as company, area, and college attended. ✎ Melissa has lost touch with a business contact who might help in setting up The Nut Tree's Web site. She remembers that her contact lives on the East Coast, but she is not sure in which state. You can use a people search site to provide Melissa with a list of people with the same name and their locations.

Steps 1234

1. Click the **Student Online Companion** link or the **Student Offline Companion** link on your home page, click the **Searching the Web folder**, then click the **Searching by people folder**

2. Click **Switchboard**
   The initial page for the Switchboard appears with options for finding a person or business, as shown in Figure C-16.

3. Click the **Find a person** link
   The Switchboard search form for finding people appears, as shown in Figure C-17. Table C-5 describes the options on this search form.

4. Click in the **First Name text box**, then type **Kim**

5. Press **[Tab]** or click in the **Last Name text box**, then type **Nickerson**
   Since you don't know the city or state where Kim lives, leave the City and State text boxes empty.

6. Click the **Search button**
   After some time, a page appears with the first 10 matches.

7. Scroll down the page, looking for East Coast addresses in the listings, then at the bottom of the page, click **Next Matches**

8. Close your browser

QuickTip

If you have even a remote idea of the state or city where someone might be living, it's better to enter your guess because it will greatly narrow the results of your search. If the search fails to locate the person, you can always search again using another state or city.

FIGURE C-16: Switchboard home page

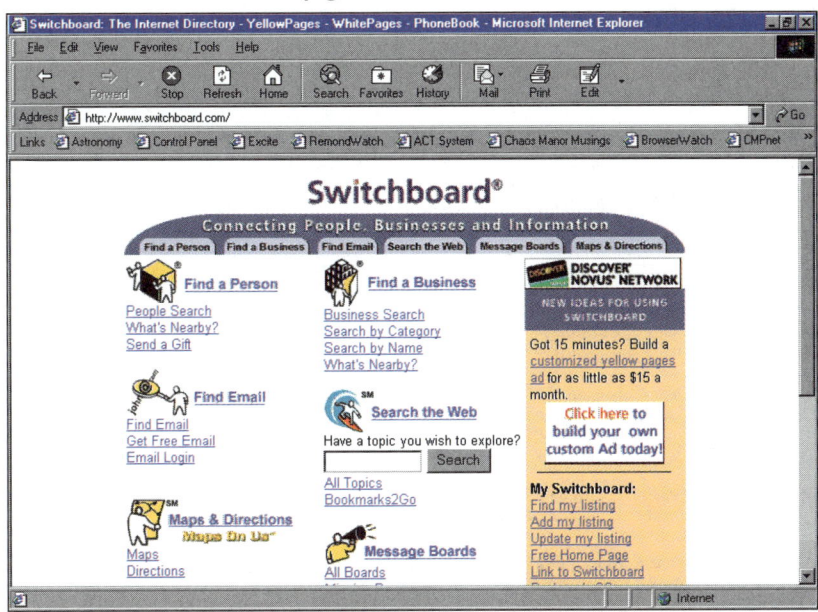

FIGURE C-17: Search form for locating people with Switchboard

City text box   State text box   Search button   Last name   First name
                                                                            text box   text box

TABLE C-5: Options in the Switchboard search form

option	description
First Name text box	Enables entry of a person's first name
Last Name text box	Enables entry of a person's last name
City text box	Allows entry of the name of the city where the person lives
State text box	Specifies the state where the person might reside
Search button	Starts the searching process

Practice

▶ Concepts Review

Briefly describe the five options of the AltaVista search form shown in Figure C-18.

FIGURE C-18

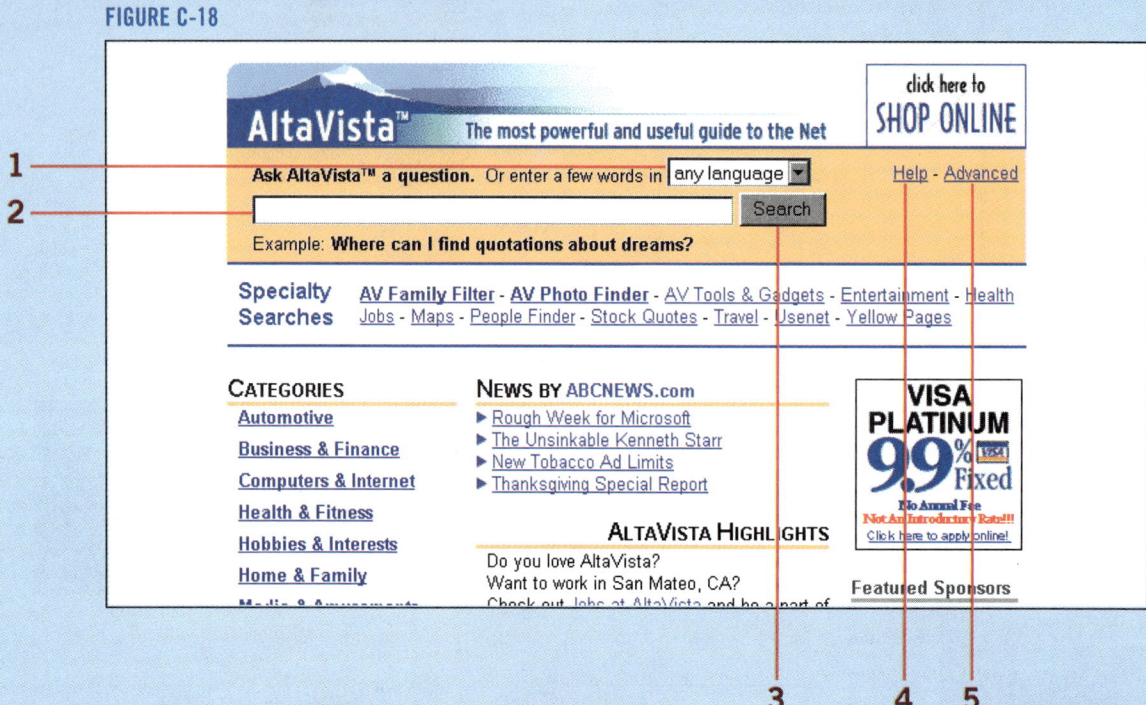

Match each term with the statement that best describes its function.

6. Yahoo!
7. Search button
8. Search Engine Watch
9. Webring
10. Switchboard

a. Pages on related subjects arranged in a circle
b. Collection
c. People finder
d. Subject directory
e. Starts the search process

Select the best answer from the list of choices.

11. Which of the following are NOT search tools?
    a. Metasearch engines
    b. Subject directories
    c. Cards
    d. Collections

12. **Which of the following is NOT a search strategy?**
    a. Search generally at first
    b. Search using a dictionary
    c. Narrow your search with search engines
    d. Browse collections

13. **Yahoo! on the Web is**
    a. A shout of joy.
    b. A location listing.
    c. A phone directory.
    d. A subject directory.

14. **Search Engine Watch is a**
    a. Webring.
    b. Collection.
    c. Companion for finding Internet protocols.
    d. Search engine.

15. **AltaVista lets you search by**
    a. Content.
    b. Latitude and longitude.
    c. Manually compiled subject directories.
    d. Webring.

16. **OnLineNow lets you search by**
    a. Collection.
    b. Index.
    c. Password.
    d. Location.

17. **The Search list box in the Dogpile search form lets you**
    a. Tell the search engines to return results for pages that match any of the words in the query.
    b. Tell the search engines to return results only for pages that contain the exact phrase specified in the query.
    c. Inform the search engines to return results only for pages that contain all of the words in the query.
    d. Determine the part of the Internet that is to be searched.

18. **A Webring consists of**
    a. Pages of content indices gathered by a spider.
    b. Related Web pages arranged in a circle for easy navigation.
    c. Lists of people.
    d. People-surfing pages.

19. **A metasearch engine works by**
    a. Querying a variety of search engine indices simultaneously.
    b. Searching a variety of metafiles at the same time.
    c. Querying the best online dictionaries.
    d. Searching for an exact phrase in a URL.

▶ Skills Review

1. **Search by subject.**
   a. Open your browser, then click either the Student Online Companion link or the Student Offline Companion link on your home page.
   b. Click the Searching the Web folder, then click the Searching by subject folder.
   c. Click InfoSpace.
   d. Click Yellow Pages.
   e. Enter "Ogden" in the City text box, click the State list arrow, choose Utah from the State list box choices, then click the Find Businesses button.
   f. Type "Gift Shops" in the Category text box, then click the Find button.
   g. Click "Gift Shops" in the Choose a category related to Gift Shops list.
   h. Examine the first 20 listings. To see more listings, click the More Results link.
   i. Return to your home page.

2. **Search by content.**
   a. Go to the Student Online Companion or the Student Offline Companion.
   b. Click the Searching the Web folder, then click the Searching by content folder.
   c. Click HotBot.
   d. Click in the Search the Web text box to display the insertion point.
   e. Type "selling nuts" (do not type the quotation marks).
   f. Click the list arrow on the text box just below, then click "exact phrase."
   g. Click the Search button.
   h. When the search results appear, scroll down the list and explore one or more of the links.
   i. Try the search again, but change the phrase to "nuts." Notice that the use of this broader term returns many more page matches.
   j. Return to your home page.

3. **Metasearch by content.**
   a. Go to the <u>Student Online Companion</u> or the <u>Student Offline Companion</u>, open the Searching the Web folder, then open the Metasearching content folder.
   b. Click <u>Metacrawler</u>.
   c. Click in the Search text box.
   d. Type "selling nuts" (do not type the quotation marks).
   e. Click the phrase option button.
   f. Click the Search button. After some time, the results appear in your document window.
   g. Explore one of the more interesting links, then return to your home page.

4. **Search by collection.**
   a. Go to the <u>Student Online Companion</u> or the <u>Student Offline Companion</u>, open the Searching the Web folder, then open the Searching by collection folder.
   b. Click <u>Browser Watch</u>.
   c. Read the most recent article or news item you can find about Web browsers.
   d. Return to your home page.

5. **Search by Webring.**
   a. Go to the <u>Student Online Companion</u> or the <u>Student Offline Companion</u>, and open the Searching the Web folder, then open the Searching by Webring folder.
   b. Click <u>Webring</u>, then click <u>Business & Economy</u>.
   c. Click <u>Electronic Commerce</u>.
   d. Scroll down, then click <u>The Internet Marketing Webring</u>.
   e. Scroll down and examine the available Webrings. Select an interesting one. Use the navigational links on the pages in the ring to travel partway around it. Be sure to take a moment and browse the information available on each page you visit.
   f. Return to your home page.

6. **Search by location.**
   a. Go to the <u>Student Online Companion</u> or the <u>Student Offline Companion</u>, and open the Searching the Web folder, then open the Searching by location folder.
   b. Click <u>Excite Travel: Regions</u>.
   c. Click the Asia region.
   d. Click on the island of Taiwan on the map.
   e. Explore some of the topics about the country.
   f. Return to your home page.

7. Search by person.

  a. Go to the <u>Student Online Companion</u> or the <u>Student Offline Companion</u>, and open the Searching the Web folder, then open the Searching by people folder.

  b. Select the 411 Locate link.

  c. Type the following name in the appropriate text boxes: Scott Adams.

  d. In the State text box, type "CA."

  e. Click the Search button.

  f. After some time, 411 Locate returns a list of people and the cities where they live.

  g. Return to the search form and try to find someone you know, using 411 Locate.

  h. Close your browser.

▶ Independent Challenges

1. You are beginning your first week as a columnist for a new magazine dedicated to covering business on the Web. You want to familiarize yourself with the current issues in electronic commerce.

  To complete this Independent Challenge:

1. From the Student Online Companion or Student Offline Companion home page, open the Searching the Web folder, then the Searching by subject folder.
2. Click <u>Yahoo!</u>, then click the <u>Business & Economy</u> category.
3. Click <u>Electronic Commerce</u>.
4. Explore two of the topics under Electronic Commerce.
5. Write a separate paragraph summarizing each subtopic to bring to the magazine's next issue-planning meeting, scheduled for later in the week.

2. A recent magazine article mentioned something called a "bot." You would like to find out what bots are and how they might help you find information on the Web.

  To complete this Independent Challenge:

1. From the Student Online Companion or Student Offline Companion home page, click the Searching the Web folder, then click the Searching by collection folder.
2. Click <u>BotSpot</u> and examine the site's homepage.
3. Click the <u>What's a bot?</u> link in the left-menu frame and read the page that appears.
4. Write a paragraph defining bots and describe how bots can help with "data mining."

3. After speaking with a Peace Corps representative and reviewing the large packet of information mailed to you, you discover you would be eligible for several teaching positions open in South Africa. You know very little about this country.

To complete this Independent Challenge:

1. From the Student Online Companion or Student Offline Companion, click the Searching the Web folder, click the Searching by Location folder, then click Excite Travel: Regions.
2. Search by location at this site to find out the following information about South Africa:
   a. The size of the country
   b. Its climate
   c. History and people
3. Write a few paragraphs summarizing the information you find.

4. John Prescott, your boss at Words and Wisdom, was very pleased with how you used the World Wide Web to help him make an informed choice about purchasing a laptop computer. He now suggests that you use the Web to find information that would help meet some of the company's other computing needs. For example, he is interested in purchasing Web server software. (*Hint*: Select the Server Watch link in the Searching by collection folder and explore the Web servers available.) Print a copy of the most interesting and appropriate Web server you find. Depending on the server you choose, your printout should look similar to the Web page shown in Figure C-19. In addition, write a brief summary of why you think this Web server is the most interesting.

FIGURE C-19

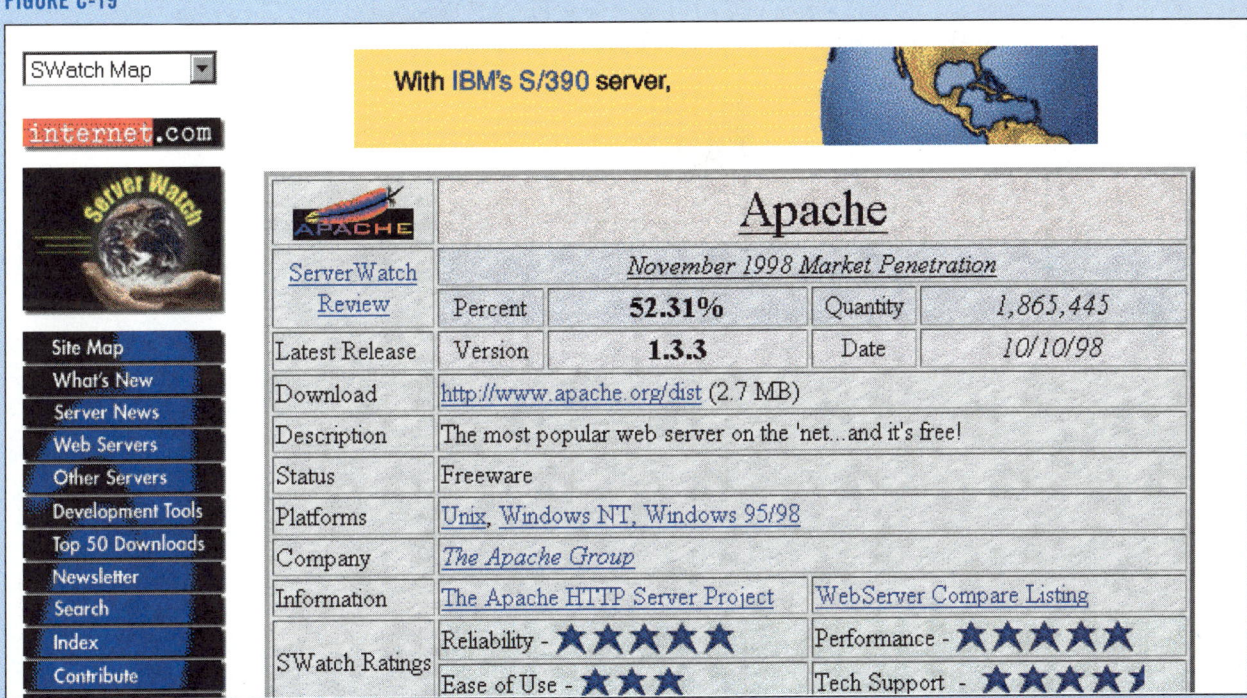

Internet

▶ Visual Workshop

Use the skills you learned in this unit to locate a Web site that sells nuts, preferably in gift packages, similar to the page shown in Figure C-20. Print a copy of the page.

FIGURE C-20

Products & Services

Santa Is On His Way...

This larger tin overflows with Roasted & Salted PECANS, Chocolate Butter Toffee PECANS, PECAN Clusters and PECAN Brittle, 8 delicious ounces of each. In this tin we have also included a large PECAN Log, a large PECAN Divinity and three Chewy Caramel PECAN Pralines. Sure to satisfy the PECAN Connoisseur.

Pecan Sampler Gift Tins

This popular SAMPLER GIFT TIN includes luscious Milk Chocolate PECANS, Roasted &

Exploring
the Web

- ► **Understand categories of information on the Web**
- ► **Explore electronic commerce**
- ► **Explore employment**
- ► **Explore electronic publishing**
- ► **Explore entertainment**
- ► **Explore government**
- ► **Explore home pages**
- ► **Explore virtual communities**

Once you know how to navigate and search the World Wide Web, it's time to explore some of the major categories of information that you can access on the Web. In this unit, you'll explore Web content in the areas of electronic commerce, employment, electronic publishing, entertainment, government, home pages, and virtual communities. You'll visit shopping malls, museums, government sites, personal home pages, and online community pages. ✎ As assistant to the marketing manager for The Nut Tree, you need to know more about the interests and desires of your potential customers so that you can better design a company Web site that appeals to Web users. To see what types of sites and information are attracting Web users, you decide to explore some of the major areas of interest on the Web. You may find some useful information for your marketing efforts as well.

Understanding Categories of Information on the Web

Understanding the organization of information on the Web is useful because it makes it easier to locate the information of interest to you. To examine the immense amount of content on the Web, you can divide it into categories, or areas of interest. Below we have listed seven of the more popular categories of interest on the Web. This list is not intended to be a comprehensive representation of what's on the Web; there are other categories of interest, such as the ones shown in Figure D-1. However, the list below describes some of the most useful and frequently visited types of sites. Exploring the following categories of information on the Web will be particularly useful as you determine how to design the Nut Tree's Web site to attract a high volume of potential customers.

 Electronic commerce: online business transactions, electronic payment systems, and online shopping

 Employment: jobs and career information

 Electronic publishing: electronic books, magazines, and newspapers

 Entertainment: art, movies, music, and TV

 Government: U.S. government directories, branches, departments, and independent establishments

 Home pages: personal pages and those of organizations

 Virtual communities: places to chat, obtain information, and exchange ideas with people who share similar interests

FIGURE D-1: Yahoo! lists additional categories of interest on the Web

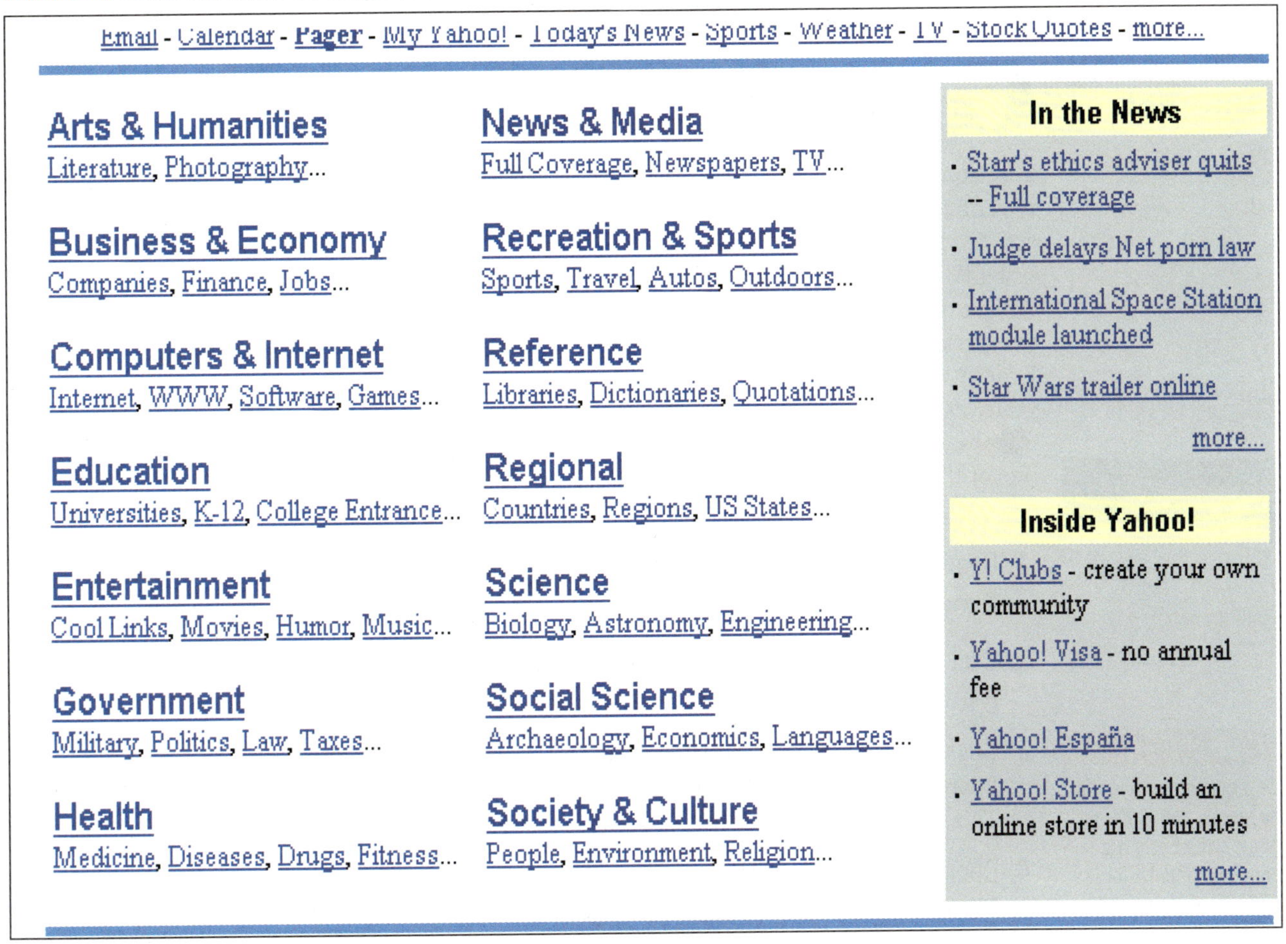

Email - Calendar - **Pager** - My Yahoo! - Today's News - Sports - Weather - TV - Stock Quotes - more...

Arts & Humanities
Literature, Photography...

Business & Economy
Companies, Finance, Jobs...

Computers & Internet
Internet, WWW, Software, Games...

Education
Universities, K-12, College Entrance...

Entertainment
Cool Links, Movies, Humor, Music...

Government
Military, Politics, Law, Taxes...

Health
Medicine, Diseases, Drugs, Fitness...

News & Media
Full Coverage, Newspapers, TV...

Recreation & Sports
Sports, Travel, Autos, Outdoors...

Reference
Libraries, Dictionaries, Quotations...

Regional
Countries, Regions, US States...

Science
Biology, Astronomy, Engineering...

Social Science
Archaeology, Economics, Languages...

Society & Culture
People, Environment, Religion...

In the News
- Starr's ethics adviser quits -- Full coverage
- Judge delays Net porn law
- International Space Station module launched
- Star Wars trailer online

more...

Inside Yahoo!
- Y! Clubs - create your own community
- Yahoo! Visa - no annual fee
- Yahoo! España
- Yahoo! Store - build an online store in 10 minutes

more...

CLUES TO USE

Web statistics and demographics

Estimates of the number of Internet users range from 40 million to 80 million, growing at a rate of 10% per month. With the exception of using e-mail, browsing the Web is by far the most popular activity on the Internet. Today, the number of Web sites totals in the millions, making available hundreds of millions of Web pages. The profiles of Web users have also changed profoundly in recent years, in terms of age, gender, and technical skills. For more information and resources on these topics, click Web statistics and demographics under the About the Web heading on the Student Online or Offline Companion.

Exploring Electronic Commerce

Electronic commerce, or **e-commerce**, is the process of transacting business online. This type of commerce primarily consists of business-to-business and business-to-consumer transactions. Both types of transactions share many concerns, such as security, electronic payment systems, and reliability. While business-to-business transactions currently represent the most dollars being spent on the Web (e.g., automobile makers purchasing parts from suppliers), business-to-consumer transactions, or **online shopping**, are rapidly growing in popularity. Experts expect online shopping to become a multibillion dollar industry over the next few years, as the convenience, the software, and the variety of retailers continue to improve. To better understand the e-commerce options for The Nut Tree, you decide to explore one of the major resources on the subject.

Steps

1. Open your browser, then click the **Student Online Companion** link on your home page or, if you are working offline, click the **Student Offline Companion** link on your home page

2. Click the **Exploring the Web folder**, then click the **Exploring electronic commerce folder**
   A list of links to e-commerce resource sites appears.

QuickTip

To see a consumer guide to online stores, click Internet Shopper in the Exploring electronic commerce folder of the Student Online Companion.

3. Click **Electronic Commerce Guide**
   Internet.com's Electronic Commerce Guide page appears, like the one shown in Figure D-2. This site offers comments from e-commerce experts, articles, resources, services, and solutions.

4. Click the link to an interesting article on the page to learn more about e-commerce
   The document window displays a page like the one shown in Figure D-3.

5. Read the article, return to the main page of the Electronic Commerce Guide and explore some of the other resources at this site

6. When you have finished, return to your home page

FIGURE D-2: Internet.com's Electronic Commerce Guide

FIGURE D-3: An article about software for building electronic storefronts

CLUES TO USE

The future of e-commerce

It's little wonder that retailers are intrigued and concerned about the Internet as a new marketing medium. Forrester Research estimates that Web sales will reach $6.6 billion by the year 2000. Killen & Associates predicts that Web sales could reach $30 billion by 2005. At the same time, Goldman Sachs has predicted that a 10%–20% switch in the retail market from local store purchasing to virtual sales could eliminate most traditional retailers' profit margins. Thus, the stakes for consumer-oriented businesses couldn't be much higher.

Unit D
Internet

Exploring Employment

The Internet has become an indispensable medium for many of today's technology-savvy job seekers and recruiters. In addition to the customary job listings section at most commercial Web sites, there are a number of sites that specialize in helping employers and job seekers find each other. Along with job-listing services, these **employment** sites typically offer assistance with career planning and resume preparation. ✎ You are looking for a creative graphic assistant to help develop the Nut Tree's Web site. You can use the Web to look for possible candidates. You decide to see how other companies list similar positions before advertising the position.

Steps

1. Click the **Student Online Companion** or **Student Offline Companion** link on your home page, click the **Exploring the Web folder**, then click the **Exploring employment folder**
   A list of links to employment sites appears.

Trouble?

If the Monster Board is unavailable, use another resource from the Exploring employment folder to look at job listings on the Web.

2. Click **Monster Board**
   The home page for the Monster Board appears, as shown in Figure D-4. The Monster Board Web site lists jobs available in the United States and internationally, with a special search agent that automatically locates positions matching your interests and qualifications. The Monster Board also provides a career center to help you hone your resume, a database to search for company information, and advice on relocation and career management.

3. Click the **Search Jobs** link
   The Job Search page displays a search form, with a number of list and text boxes.

4. Scroll down in the Location Search list box until **Washington-Seattle** appears, then click it
   The Washington-Seattle selection appears highlighted. Once you've chosen an area in which to look for job listings, you want to narrow your search to a specific type of job.

5. Scroll down in the Profession Search list box until **Creative Arts/Media** appears, then click it
   The category selection appears highlighted, as shown in Figure D-5.

Trouble?

If no positions are currently available in the chosen location, return to the search form, click another location (e.g., California-San Jose), then repeat the search.

6. Scroll down the page, then click the **Search Jobs button**
   The results appear on a new page, similar to Figure D-6.

7. Scroll down to see the list of positions found

8. Click one of the job postings
   A page with information about a job listing appears.

9. Examine the information that is available for the position (e.g., duties, responsibilities, and qualifications)

QuickTip

Use the Keyword Search text box to look for types of jobs not listed in the Category Search list box.

10. Go back to the results list and explore some of the other postings, then return to your home page

FIGURE D-4: Monster Board

Job Search link ——

FIGURE D-5: Both list boxes show the correctly highlighted items

First selection ——

Second selection ——

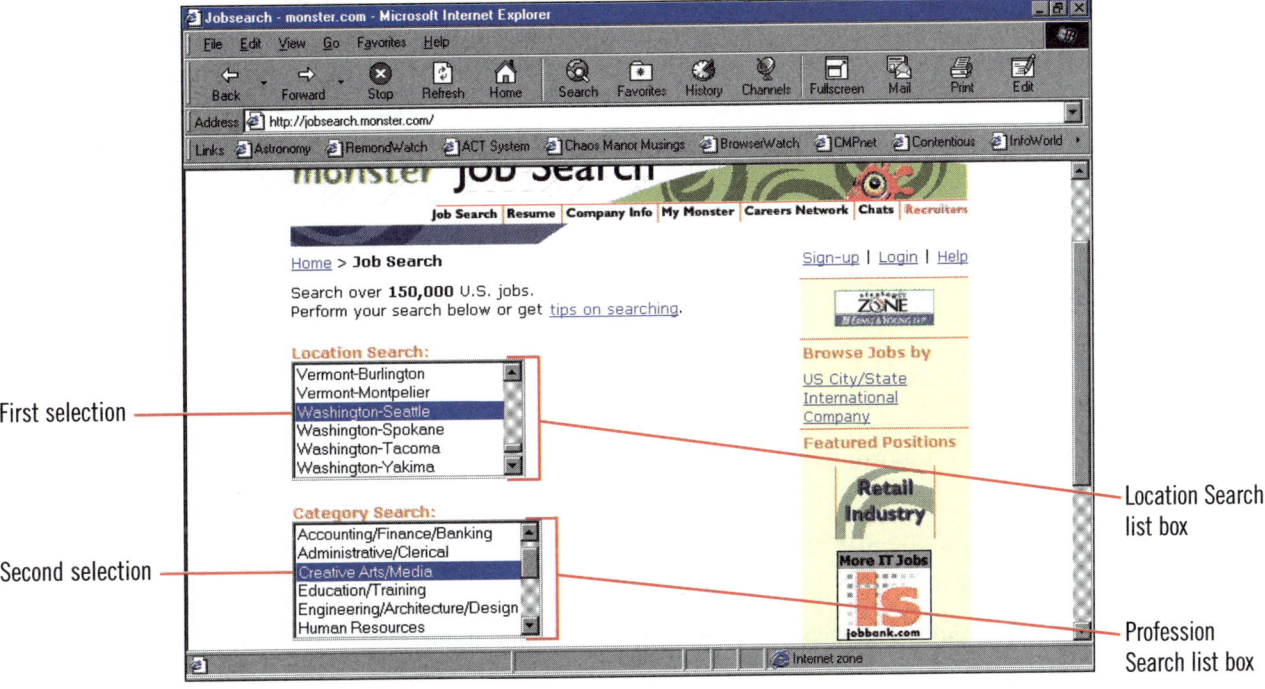

Location Search list box

Profession Search list box

FIGURE D-6: Example of search results

Results list ——

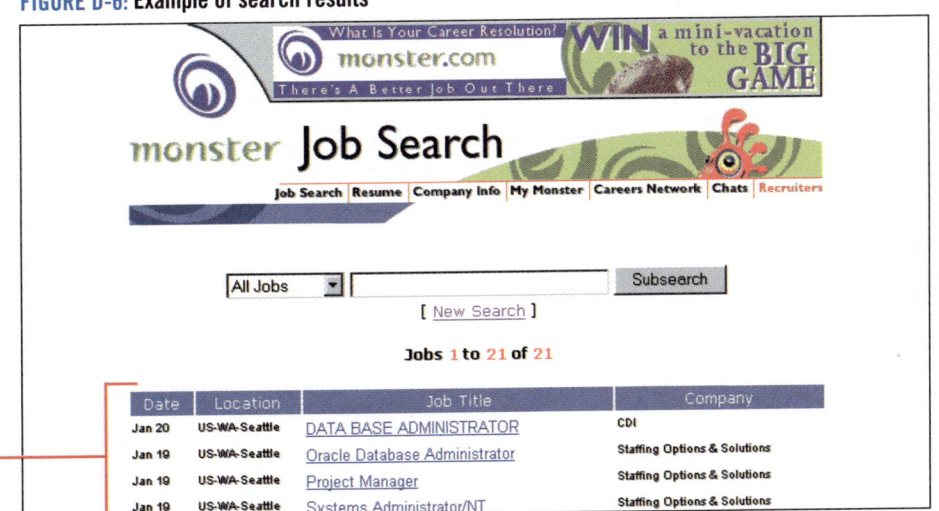

Exploring Electronic Publishing

The number of electronic publishers on the Web is growing all the time. New electronic books, newspapers, and magazines appear almost daily, although some eventually become economic failures. With growing competition from online news sources, almost every major (and many small-city) print newspapers have begun to offer part, or all, of their content on the Web in order to retain revenues from their classified advertisements. In book publishing, the list of electronic books online is impressive (with many classic works available), but the real growth in this medium will occur when eye fatigue from reading lengthy text is lessened by advances in computer display technology. Electronic magazines are the most popular electronic publishing medium because they typically incorporate interesting images along with brief but insightful articles. Many of these electronic magazines discuss business and lifestyle issues for those who work and play in cyberspace whereas others focus on the technology issues of the Web. Some electronic magazines are simply Web versions of magazines that also exist in print form, and include many or all of the same articles found in the printed versions. Other electronic magazines, however, are found only on the Web. You want to investigate an electronic magazine that covers the business side of the Internet to gain a better appreciation of the industry.

Steps

1. Click the <u>Student Online Companion</u> or <u>Student Offline Companion</u> link on your home page, click the **Exploring the Web folder**, then click the **Exploring electronic publishing folder**

2. Click <u>The Industry Standard</u>
   The home page for The Industry Standard appears, as shown in Figure D-7.

3. Click the **Opinion link** on the menu to the left
   A list of columns appears in the right frame, like the ones shown in Figure D-8.

4. Scroll down, then click the link for an article from the list
   Your document window displays the article, like the one pictured in Figure D-9.

5. Read the article, return to the Opinion index page, then click the link for another article that looks interesting to you

6. Read the article, then return to your home page

FIGURE D-7: The Industry Standard home page

Opinion link →

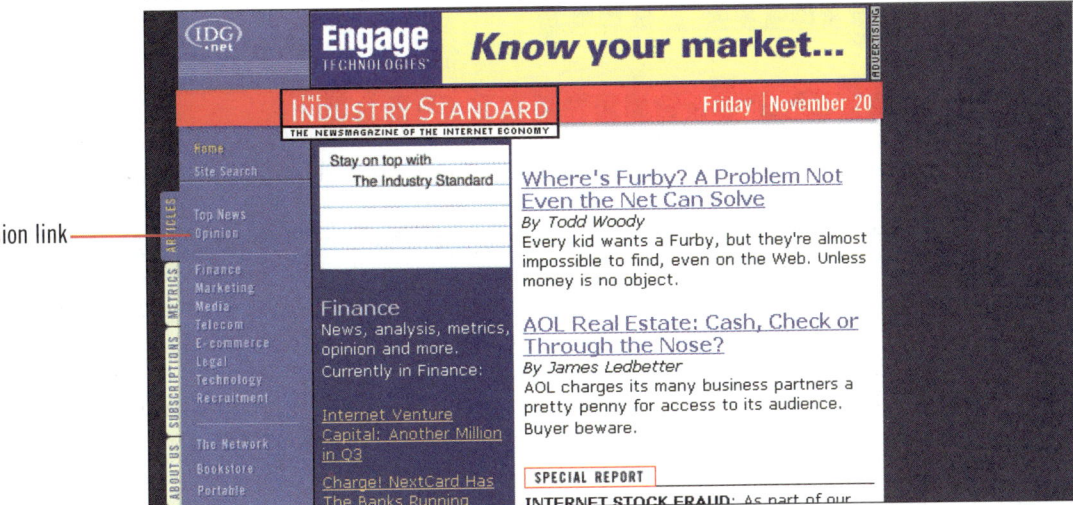

FIGURE D-8: Sample list of opinion columns

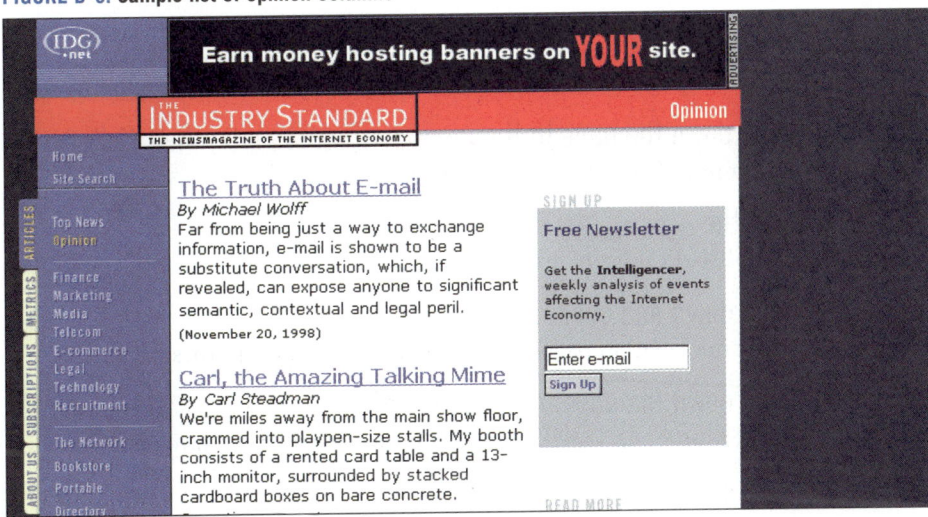

FIGURE D-9: Sample opinion column

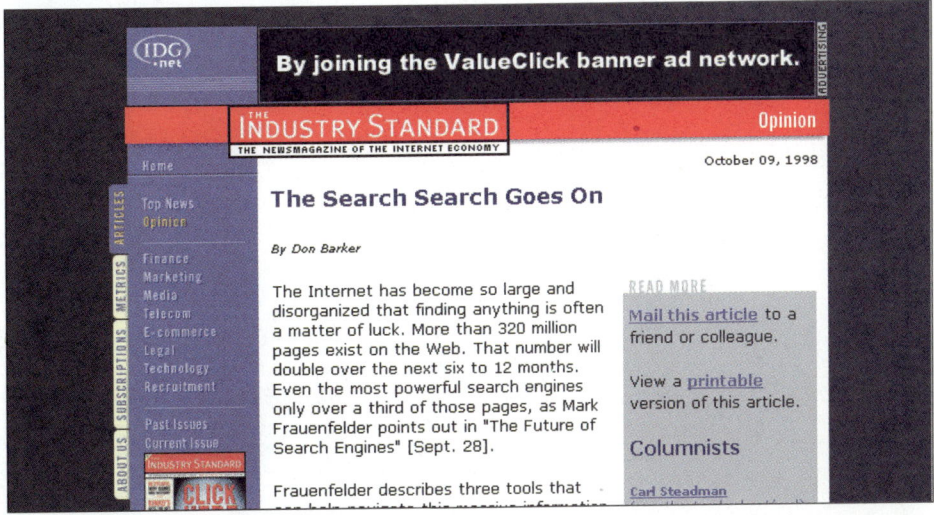

Unit D

Internet

Exploring Entertainment

The interactive nature of the Web lets you have lots of fun and be highly entertained. Virtual art collections, galleries, and museums are some of the more eye-catching and inspiring sites to tour on the Web. They feature breathtaking digital representations of the world's greatest pieces of artwork. In addition, the Web provides an almost endless variety of other entertainment options. There are promotional movie sites stocked with film-related goodies such as downloadable posters and video clips, music hangouts where you can discuss and listen to your favorite bands, and articles and schedules for your favorite TV shows, to name just a few. To keep visitors coming back to your company Web site, you want to make it entertaining as well as informative and helpful. So, you decide to visit a popular entertainment site on the Web.

Steps 123 4

1. Click the **Student Online Companion** or **Student Offline Companion** link on your home page, click the **Exploring the Web folder**, then click the **Exploring entertainment folder**

QuickTip

To increase the speed at which images load, scroll down to the bottom of this page and select a WebMuseum site closest to your location.

2. Click **WebMuseum**
   The home page for the WebMuseum appears, as shown in Figure D-10.

3. Scroll down the page to the **Famous Painting link**, then click it
   The Famous Painting exhibition page opens

4. Click the **Artist Index link**
   An alphabetical list of artists appears.

5. Scroll down and click the link **Leonardo da Vinci**
   An art information page about Leonardo da Vinci appears.

6. Scroll down the page to the image of **"The Adoration of the Magi"**
   A collection of da Vinci's paintings become visible, as shown in Figure D-11.

7. Click on the image of **"The Adoration of the Magi"** to load a larger representation of the painting
   After a time, your document window fills with the larger representation, as shown in Figure D-12. You will need to use your scroll bars (or print it) to view the entire piece of artwork.

8. When you have finished, return to your home page

FIGURE D-10: WebMuseum home

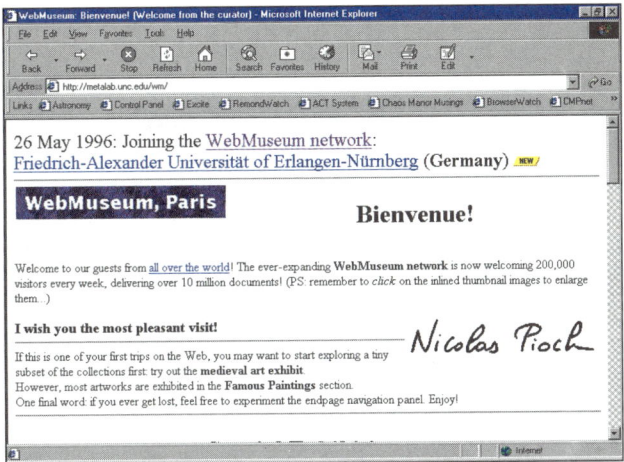

FIGURE D-11: A collection of Leonardo da Vinci's painting

The Adoration
of the Magi

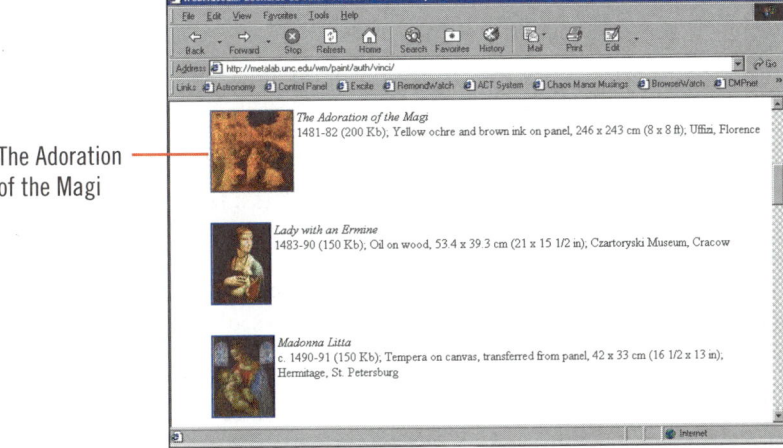

FIGURE D-12: The Adoration of the Magi by Leonardo da Vinci

Print the entire
painting to see
it in its entirety

Use scroll bars to
view different
portions of the
painting

CLUES TO USE

Web ethics and law

The question of Web developers' responsibilities and rights regarding the content they make available on their Web sites is an ongoing debate. This question is both an ethical and legal one. For information on the ethical issues, click the About the Web folder in the Student Online or Offline Companion, click the Ethics folder, then click one of the links. To find out about bills affecting these legal issues, click the Exploring the Web folder, click the Exploring government folder, then click Thomas. Use the Thomas site to search for bills pending or passed about online copyrights and other Web content issues.

Exploring Government

The U.S. government continues to establish services on the Web at such a rapid rate that it is sometimes hard to find the exact site you want. Table D-1 briefly describes how the federal government is organized on the Web. Fortunately, the government provides a number of subject directory and search engine sites to assist in locating information within the federal bureaucracy. You want to explore the business help that is available from U.S. government Web sites. You are especially interested in resources that will help you plan your expansion of The Nut Tree's business into cyberspace.

Steps

1. Click the **Student Online Companion** or **Student Offline Companion** link on your home page, click the **Exploring the Web folder**, then click the **Exploring government folder**

2. Click **U.S. Business Advisor**
The home page for U.S. Business Advisor opens, as shown in Figure D-13. You want to gain an overview of the types of resources and online services that are available from the government.

3. Scroll down to review the page, then click the **Browse button** toward the top of the page
The Welcome to Browse page opens. This page offers a table with a link to each main topic.

4. Scroll down, then click **General Business**
The General Business page opens, as shown in Figure D-14. This page provides categories of links related to general business topics. You want to see what kind of publications and contacts are available to assist you.

5. Scroll down, then click **Publications/Contacts**, or scroll down the page manually to the heading **Publications and Contacts**
A list of online government publications and contacts appears.

6. Click **SBA Advocacy Corner [SBA]**
The SBA Advocacy Corner page appears, with a list of links to information discussing important items of concern to small business, as shown in Figure D-15.

7. When you have finished, return to your home page

Trouble?
If you cannot connect to the U.S. Business Advisor, skip the following steps, click another link from the Exploring the government folder (such as FedWorld), and look there for government resources for business.

TABLE D-1: Selected federal government resources on the Web

type of federal site	examples
Branch	1. Executive Branch (White House speeches) 2. Legislative Branch (Congressional bills) 3. Judicial
Department	4. U.S. Department of Commerce (information on international trade and commerce) 5. U.S. Department of Defense (military-related information) 6. U.S. Department of Labor (labor statistics)
Independent establishment	7. Small Business Administration (SBA) (small-business-related information) 8. Federal Bureau of Investigation (FBI) (the Ten Most Wanted list and other information about federal crime) 9. U.S. Census Bureau (U.S. census data plus other statistical sources)

FIGURE D-13: U.S. Business Advisor

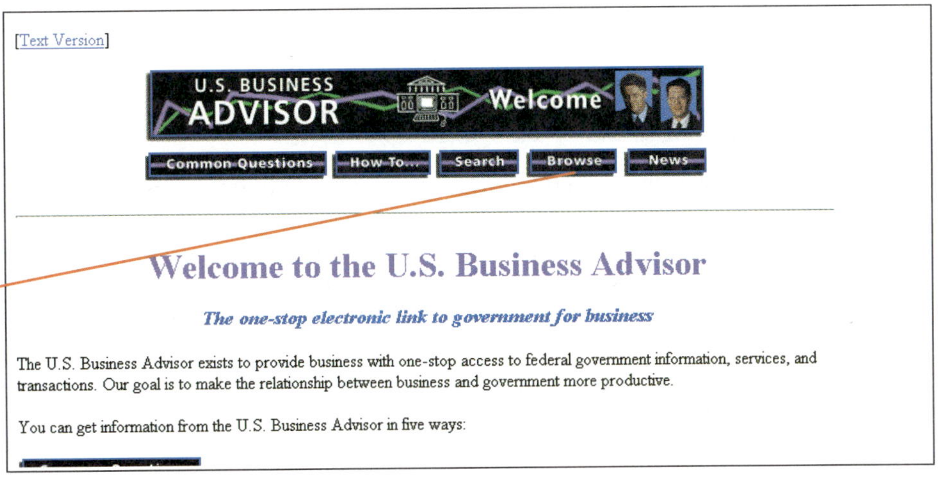

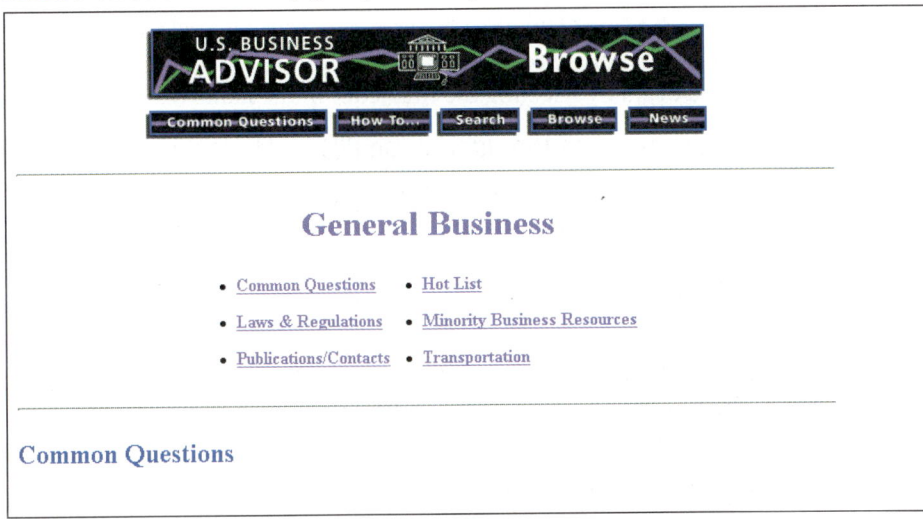

Browse button—
displays an
alphabetical
directory of
government sites
that offer
resources for
business

FIGURE D-14: General Business page of pointers to government commerce information

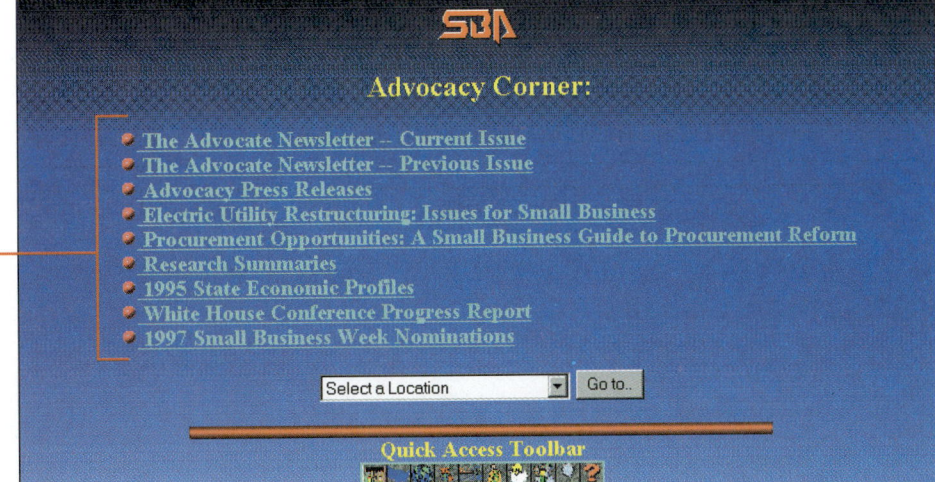

FIGURE D-15: SBA Advocacy Corner page

Links to
newsletters,
reports, and
guides

Unit D
Internet

Exploring Home Pages

The Web contains home pages for both individuals and organizations. Personal home pages are typically very innovative and therefore fun to view. They can also serve as a great source of new ideas for developing unique and attractive company home pages. Although no official rules exist for judging the quality of a home page, Table D-2 describes some general characteristics shared by many of the most popular home pages. Keep these characteristics in mind as you view different home pages on the Web. ✎ Melissa, now convinced that the Web represents a real business opportunity for The Nut Tree, asks you to design a home page for the company. As a first step, you'll visit a variety of home pages to gather innovative design ideas.

Steps 1 2 3 4

1. Click the **Student Online Companion** link or **Student Offline Companion** link on your home page, click the **Exploring the Web folder**, then click the **Exploring home pages folder**

2. Click **Student.com**
   The initial page for Student.com opens, as shown in Figure D-16. Student.com offers a large collection of individual home pages. You can locate individual student home pages by their schools. You begin by selecting the first letter in the name of the student's school.

3. Click the list arrow on the right of the PICK A LETTER list box, scroll down if necessary through the drop-down list that appears, then click the first letter in the name of the school you want to search (e.g., "W" for "Walla Walla College")

4. Click the **Go There** button
   A list of schools starting with the selected letter appears.

5. Click on a link to a school of your choice (e.g., Walla Walla College)
   Most schools offer a list of names to browse, although some provide search forms to locate a particular home page.

6. Look over the school's list of personal home pages, then click one of the links to view a page
   A home page appears, like the one shown in Figure D-17.

7. Explore this page, then go back and explore one or two other home pages

8. When you have finished, return to your home page

FIGURE D-16: Student.com

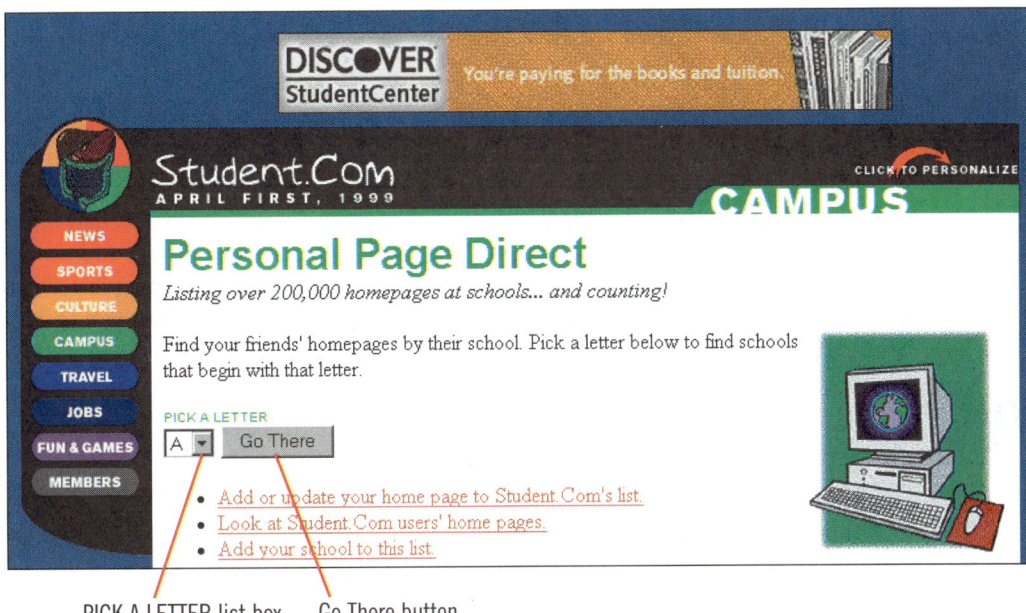

PICK A LETTER list box   Go There button

FIGURE D-17: Sample personal home page

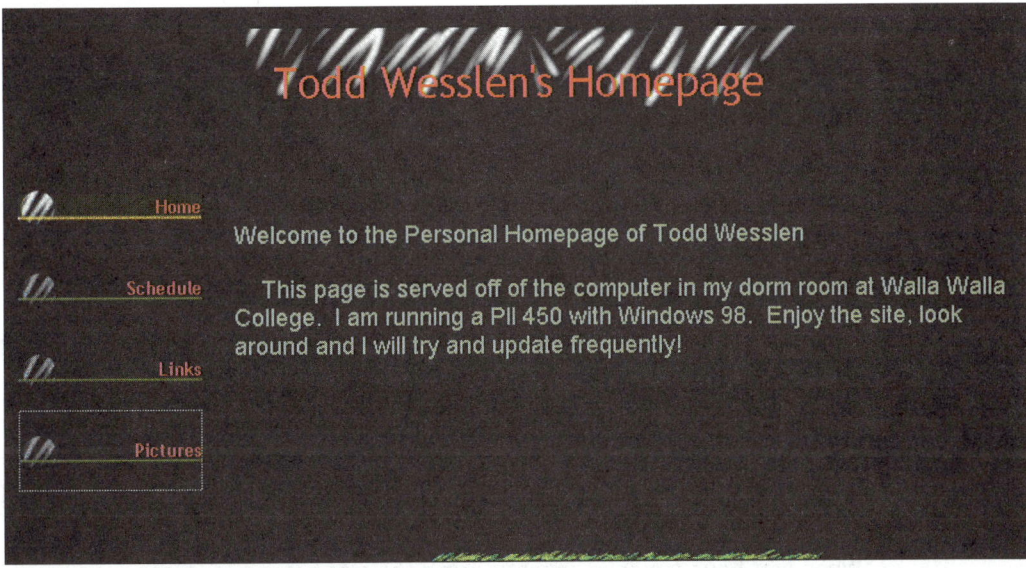

TABLE D-2: Characteristics of a good home page

include	don't include
Innovative and eye-catching images	Large images on the home page—bloated images slow loading and, thus, discourage visitors from returning
Unique and valuable information	Long, cluttered, or wordy pages
Short and to-the-point Web pages	Nonfunctioning or outdated links
Links to other related pages on the Web	Links to large files without labels or warnings about their size—users don't want to wait long periods to navigate your site
Warnings advising viewers of the size of the file	Obscure or hard-to-read icons (for example, still images, sound files, and video clips)
Meaningful buttons and icons to help users quickly and easily find the desired information	Scattered or random assortment of confusing buttons or impossible-to-comprehend icons

Exploring Virtual Communities

A **virtual community** is a site in cyberspace where people gather to discuss topics of mutual interest, make friends, and form groups that will stay in contact over time. Like any healthy community, a good virtual community provides its members with support and advice. It can also lessen the isolation of cyberspace by providing meeting places where people on the cutting edge of the information age can share their experiences. ✒️ Melissa asks you to explore a virtual community to see what support and resources might be available to help both of you better understand this new medium.

Steps

1. Click the <u>**Student Online Companion**</u> or <u>**Student Offline Companion**</u> link on your home page, click the **Exploring the Web folder**, then click the **Exploring virtual communities folder**

2. Click **The WELL**
   The home page for The WELL appears, as shown in Figure D-18. Virtual communities like The WELL often offer conferences (discussions), home pages, and e-mail accounts for their members.

3. Click **Conferencing** at the top of the WELL home page
   A page describing the conferences at The WELL appears.

4. Scroll down the page, then click **Conference Directory**
   A page displaying a list of conferences (discussions) appears, as shown in Figure D-19.

5. Click a particular conference topic, such as **Computers & Internet Conferences**
   A page listing ongoing conferences appears, as shown in Figure D-20.

6. Examine the discussion topics to get a feel for the computer and Internet topics people are discussing
   Most virtual communities, like The WELL, require that you become a member before you can actually join a conference or access their resources and activities. Some sites require membership fees, whereas others are supported by advertising and corporate sponsorships and offer free registration.

7. When you have finished investigating the site offerings, close your browser

FIGURE D-18: Initial page for The WELL

Conferencing link

FIGURED-19: Directory of conferences at The WELL

Computers & Internet Conferences

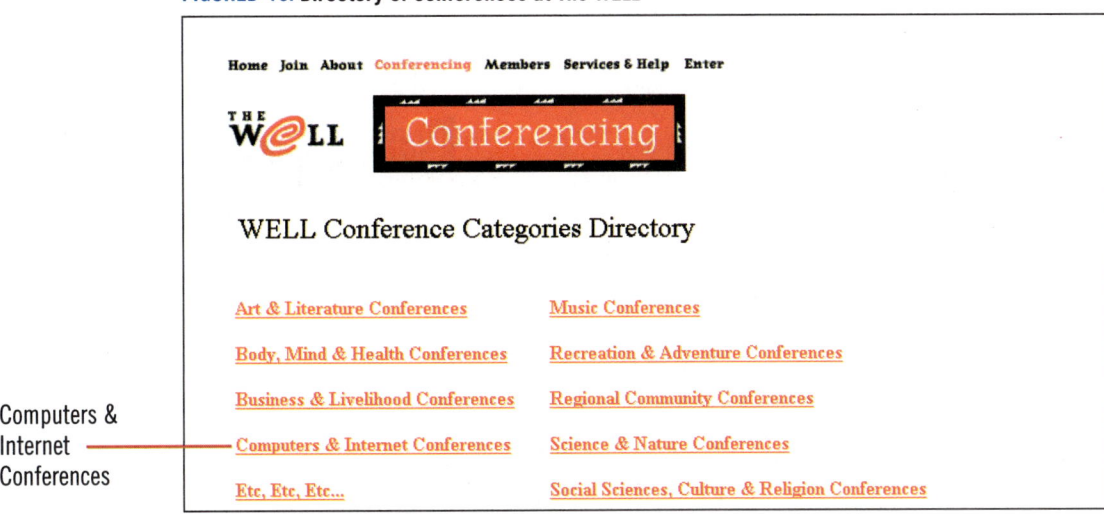

FIGURE D-20: List of Computer and the Internet related conferences

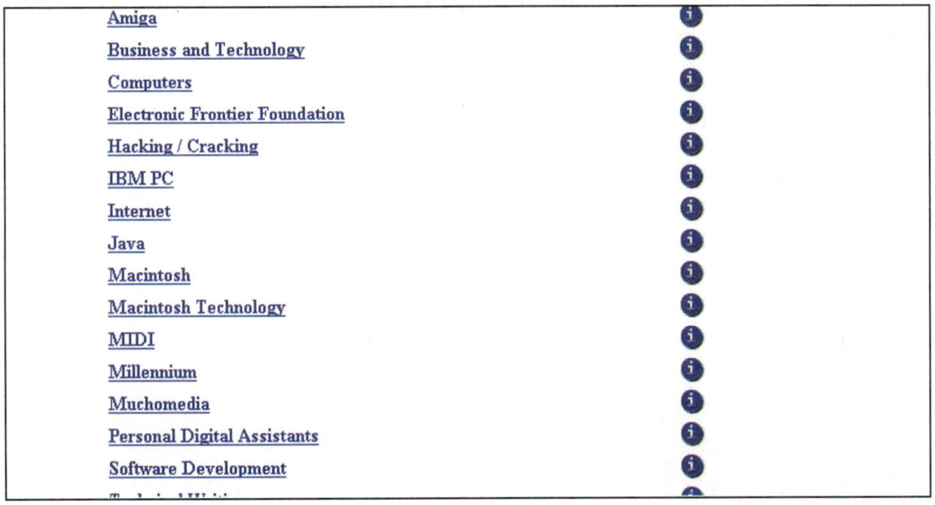

Amiga

Business and Technology

Computers

Electronic Frontier Foundation

Hacking / Cracking

IBM PC

Internet

Java

Macintosh

Macintosh Technology

MIDI

Millennium

Muchomedia

Personal Digital Assistants

Software Development

Practice

► Concepts Review

Label the characteristics of a good personal home page indicated in Figure D-21.

FIGURE D-21

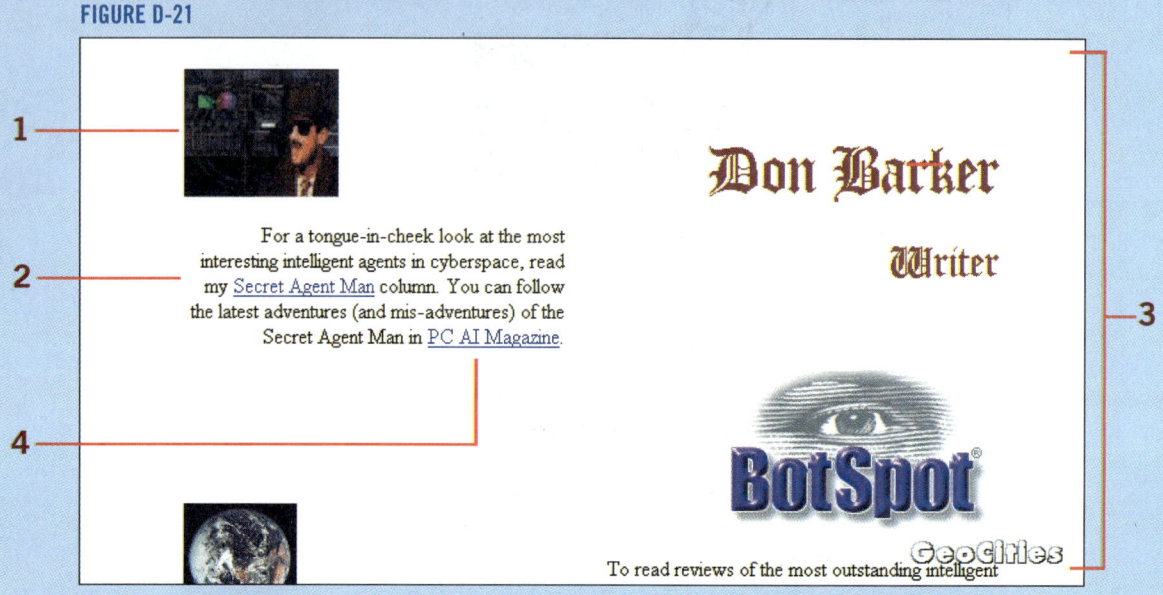

Match each of the terms below with the statement that best describes its function.

5. Electronic commerce
6. The Industry Standard
7. U.S. Business Advisor
8. ArtNet
9. Student.com

a. Electronic magazine
b. Government service
c. Contains individual home pages
d. Transacting business online
e. Directory of art and art resources

Select the best answer from the list of choices.

10. The following are all areas of interest for electronic publishing on the Web, except
    a. Electronic books.
    b. Electronic newspapers.
    c. Electronic magazines.
    d. Electronic posters.

11. Which of the following is NOT a federal government category?
    a. Department
    b. Office
    c. Branch
    d. Not for profit

12. Which of the following is NOT a characteristic of a good home page?
    a. Short length and concise writing
    b. Large graphics
    c. Links to related resources
    d. Innovative and eye-catching images

13. The growth rate of the number of Web users is
    a. 5% per month.
    b. 10% per month.
    c. 5% per year.
    d. 10% per year.

14. Which of the following is NOT a reason why a Web page may take a long time to load?
    a. A large graphical image appears on the page
    b. High traffic on the Internet
    c. The speed of your connection to the Internet
    d. The length of your monitor's AC cord

15. U.S. Business Advisor is
    a. A searchable subject directory and index with links to government business resources.
    b. A commercial computer game.
    c. The Web site for the Budget Office.
    d. A government-produced game about the state of the economy.

16. Which category would you select if you want to find a listing of electronic books?
    a. Home pages
    b. Electronic publishing
    c. Business
    d. Government

Internet

17. Which is the subject of many of today's most popular electronic magazines?
   a. Electronic commerce
   b. Facials
   c. Skiing
   d. Roller-skating

18. A virtual community is a
   a. 1960s communal style of living.
   b. Group of people who share common interests, become friends, and form groups over time.
   c. Group of people who refuse to use technology.
   d. Collection of people who surf the Web without direction.

 # Skills Review

1. Explore electronic commerce.
   a. Go to the Student Online Companion or the Student Offline Companion, click the Exploring the Web folder, then click the Exploring electronic commerce folder.
   b. Click Internet Shopper.
   c. Scroll down the page, type "nuts" in the Find a product text box, then click the Search button.
   d. When the search results appear, scroll down, click a link to a retailer of nuts, then explore the site.
   e. Return to your home page.

2. Explore employment.
   a. Go to the Student Online Companion or the Student Offline Companion, click the Exploring the Web folder, then click the Exploring employment folder.
   b. Click CareerMosaic.
   c. Click the Search Jobs icon.
   d. When the search form appears, type "Web developer" in the Job Title text box.
   e. Type "Seattle" in the City text box, then click the Search Now! button.
   f. Explore the search results. (*Note*: If no Web developer positions are available for Seattle, return to the search form and enter another city, such as Los Angeles.)
   g. Return to your home page.

3. **Explore electronic publishing.**
   a. Go to the Student Online Companion or the Student Offline Companion, and click the Exploring the Web folder, then click the Exploring electronic publishing folder.
   b. Click HotWired.
   c. Find and read a news article on the HotWired page that interests you.
   d. Return to your home page.

4. **Explore entertainment.**
   a. Go to the Student Online Companion or the Student Offline Companion, and click the Exploring the Web folder, then click the Exploring entertainment folder.
   b. Click The Internet Movie Database.
   c. Type "Wizard of Oz" in the Search for title/name text box, then click the Go button.
   d. Explore the results to find out who directed the 1939 release of *The Wizard of Oz*.
   e. Return to your home page.

5. **Explore government.**
   a. Go to the Student Online Companion or the Student Offline Companion, and click the Exploring the Web folder, then click the Exploring government folder.
   b. Click Thomas.
   c. Find and click in the Search by Word/Phrase text box, type "Internet", then click the Search button.
   d. Explore one of the bills listed in the search results.
   e. Return to your home page.

6. **Explore home pages.**
   a. Go to the Student Online Companion or the Student Offline Companion, and click the Exploring the Web folder, then click the Exploring home pages folder.
   b. Click Student.com.
   c. Click Look at Student.Com users' home pages.
   d. Click a letter in the PICK A LETTER list box, then click the Go There button.
   e. Scroll down the list, then click the link to someone's home page.
   f. Return to the list of home pages and visit another one.
   g. Return to your home page.

7. Explore virtual communities.

  a. Go to the <u>Student Online Companion</u> or the <u>Student Offline Companion</u>, and click the Exploring the Web folder, then click the Exploring virtual communities folder.

  b. Click a virtual community link (for example, <u>The Globe</u>).

  c. Examine the topics of conversation and types of activities available at this site.

  d. Close your browser.

▶ Independent Challenges

1. The PR firm Words and Wisdom is growing rapidly. John Prescott realizes that he needs to be able to conduct business online. He asks you to find out more about electronic payment systems.

  To complete this Independent Challenge:

1. Go to the Student Online or Offline Companion.
2. Click the Exploring the Web folder, then click the Exploring electronic commerce folder.
3. Click <u>E-Commerce Watch</u>.
4. Read one of the news stories about e-commerce.
5. Write two paragraphs summarizing the story.

2. Your American history professor has assigned research topics for the final paper. Your paper will discuss the history of the White House. You decide to use the Web to research your paper.

  To complete this Independent Challenge:

1. Go to the Student Online or Offline Companion.
2. Click the Exploring the Web folder, then click the Exploring government folder.
3. Click <u>White House</u>.
4. Click <u>White House History and Tours</u>, then explore this site.
5. Print a copy of the White House's home page to include with your research paper.

3. You have applied to and been accepted by an art school in Paris, France, and you leave next month. You want to familiarize yourself with art galleries in Paris before you leave. Use the ArtNet link in the Exploring entertainment folder to learn more about art galleries in Paris. Print a copy of the most interesting gallery you find.

4. An instructor wants to teach her students how to create their own home pages, so she searches for an example of a page that has a good balance of text and clean graphics. Use the Exploring home pages folder links to find and print two Web pages: (1) a well-designed page and (2) a page that could use some work. Describe how the second page could be improved. (Be sure to use the characteristics listed in Table D-2 in your description.)

▶ Visual Workshop

Use the skills you learned in this unit to find and print the digitized painting shown in Figure D-22.

FIGURE D-22

Internet

Glossary

Address Unique string of text that identifies the location of a Web page on the World Wide Web. Also known as the Uniform Resource Locator (URL).

Address bar Displays URL for current Web page, and allows entry of a URL to open in the document window. *See also* Uniform Resource Locator (URL).

Boolean operators Special connecting words (i.e. AND, OR, and NOT) that indicate the relationship among keywords in a Web search statement.

Cache A file of saved Web pages.

Collection Compiled by individuals or organizations to offer information and links to Web sites related to a particular subject. *See also* Guide.

Content-oriented search A search method which is most effective when searching for information on a specific topic. Requires a search engine. *See also* search engine.

Document window Displays the current Web page. *See also* Web page.

Domain name The part of a URL indicating the Web site name and extension. For example, in the URL www.microsoft.com, the domain name is microsoft.com. *See also* Uniform Resource Locator (URL) and Web site.

Electronic mail (e-mail) A system used to send and receive messages electronically.

Electronic commerce The selling and marketing of goods and services via the Internet.

Electronic publishers Organizations that provide hypertext books, magazines, and newspapers online.

Explorer bar A collection of buttons and controls to help the user easily maneuver around the Web. The bar is displayed on the left side while the current Web page is displayed on the right side of the browser window.

Favorite The name and address of a Web page stored in the user's collection of favorite Web pages.

Favorites list A feature of Internet Explorer that enables the user to collect and organize the names and addresses of favorite Web pages (or sites) for quick and easy access in the future.

File Transfer Protocol (FTP) A communication standard that allows users to retrieve and send files over the Internet.

Formatting tag A type of HTML tag that provides control over how Web pages are displayed in a Web browser (e.g. bold or italics). *See also* Hypertext Markup Language.

Frames Divide the document window into numerous smaller windows, each containing unique information. This feature can display new pages in one or more frames while maintaining the same information in other frames.

FrontPage Express An HTML editor for creating Web pages that provides easy to use features to modify, format, enhance, and publish Web presentations. No knowledge of HTML is necessary as FrontPage Express offers a friendly WYSIWYG environment.

Global domain The last letters of a domain name that indicate the category a Web site belongs to. For example, the global name extension .edu indicates that the Web site is part of the educational domain on the Internet. Also known as a top level domain.

Graphic *See* image.

Groupware Software that enables electronic collaboration between users.

Guide Compiled by individuals or organizations to offer information and links to Web sites related to a particular subject. *See also* Collection.

Guided Tour A navigational aid that lists and describes new, unusual, and outstanding Web pages.

Home page The initial Web page that loads each time you launch a Web browser. The term is also used to refer to the main page of a Web site. *See also* Web page.

Horizontal scroll bar Allows users to quickly move left and right through a Web page.

Hypertext links, hyperlinks Web page elements that enable the user to open related Web pages by clicking them with the mouse.

Hypertext Markup Language (HTML) The programming language used to describe the general structure of a Web page. HTML uses special characters, called tags, to enable browsers to properly display the contents of a Web page. *See also* structuring tags and formatting tags.

Hypertext Transfer Protocol (HTTP) The communication standard established for the World Wide Web that ensures every computer accessing the World Wide Web is using the same language when sending and receiving Web pages.

Icon A symbol used to represent a command.

Image An electronic file of a drawing, picture, or almost any static illustration.

Image map A graphic containing multiple links. *See also* Image.

Index A list of keywords with links to the pages they appear on as compiled by a search engine. *See also* Search Engine.

Insertion Point A blinking vertical line in the document window of an editor that indicates where any new text will appear. Also known as a cursor.

Instance Each is a separate Internet Explorer window, complete with all toolbars and menus, in which the user can navigate independently from the other instance.

Internet A collection of networks that connects computers all over the world together using phone lines, fiber optic cables, satellites, and other telecommunications media. *See also* network.

Internet e-mail address Used to send someone mail electronically, it consists of the recipient's user name, the @ symbol, and the domain name of the host (mail server).

Internet Explorer A program, developed by Microsoft, known as a Web browser that allows the user to interact with the World Wide Web. *See also* Web Browser.

Intranet A network, or networks, that uses Internet standards but is restricted to the members of a particular group or organization. *See also* network.

Keyword(s) Words entered into a search form to locate content on the Web that matches. *See also* search form.

Links Web page elements that enable the user to open related Web pages by clicking them. Also known as hyperlinks.

Links toolbar Offers a predefined set of buttons leading to interesting and useful sites on the Web.

Load a Web page Refers to the process of opening a Web page. *See also* hyperlink.

Location directories and maps Search tool on the Web that allows the user to specify a geographical region in which to look for information.

Location-oriented search A search method often conducted using maps. This method is best used when attempting to locate Web sites in a specific geographical area. *See also* Web site and map.

Map A search tool that displays locations of Web sites geographically. This type of search tool works well when searching for Web sites in a particular geographical region.

Menu bar Displays the names of the menus that contain commands. Clicking a menu name on the menu bar displays a list of commands from which you can choose.

Metasearch engines Single forms for querying multiple search engine indices simultaneously when searching the Web based on keywords or phrases.

Navigate To move between Web sites.

NetMeeting A real-time audio/video communication program that enables the user to speak with and see another person over the Internet or within an intranet. The program also permits you to share and work with drawings, worksheets, and graphics during a conference, regardless of the participants' locations.

Network Two or more computers connected together in order to exchange data and share resources.

Offline The status of not being connected to the Web.

Online The status of being connected to the Web.

Online libraries Provide collections of publications in an electronic form easily accessible to users.

Online Shopping Online business transactions where consumers purchase goods and/or services.

Outlook Express A combined e-mail program and news-group reader that allows the user to send, receive, and manage messages, and participate in newsgroup discussions.

People Search site Search tool for the Web that locates people.

Progress bar Center box on the Status bar that visually indicates the status of a Web page's loading process by filling in with a blue bar.

Relevancy Scores Ratings of how close search results match a query to a search engine.

RingWorld The subject directory where the user searches or browses for a Webring about a particular subject. *See also* Webring, Subject directory.

Scroll box A small square-shaped control, located in the vertical and horizontal scroll bars, that lets the user quickly move through a long document and indicates the relative position in the document. *See also* horizontal scroll bar and vertical scroll bar.

Search engine A Web site that uses entries in a search form to scan for relevant information stored in an index of the Web. *See also* search form.

Search form A Web page that enables the user to specify what information a search engine should look for. *See also* search engine.

Secured site Refers to any Web site that uses encrypted transmissions and takes other appropriate measures to ensure the protection of sensitive information such as credit card information.

Spider A computer program used by search engines to index the contents of Web pages at each site as it travels from one site to another.

Standard Button Toolbar Contains icons that function as shortcuts to frequently used Internet Explorer menu commands.

Status bar Displays important information about the current operation, such as the percentage loaded of a Web page's layout and graphics. *See also* load a Web page.

Status Indicator (the Internet Explorer logo) Indicates the status of loading a Web page in the document window. The indicator becomes animated as a new page is loading; when it stops moving, the page loading process is complete.

Structuring tag A type of HTML tag that marks the element of a Web page, such as the title, head, and body, used to organize the elements of a Web page. *See also* Hypertext Markup Language.

Subject directory A list of links to general information topics, arranged alphabetically to facilitate browsing.

Subject-oriented search Type of search effective in finding general or broad information. *See also* subject directory.

Surfing the Web Refers to the activity of randomly or intentionally selecting the links found in Web pages to travel, or navigate, about the Web. *See also* hyperlinks.

Title bar Displays the title of the current Web page at the top of the application window.

Top level domain or extension The last letters of a domain name that indicate the category a Web site belongs to. For example, the global name extension .edu indicates that the Web site is part of the educational domain on the Internet. Also known as global domain.

Internet

Uniform Resource Locator (URL) Unique string of text that identifies the location of a Web page on the World Wide Web. Also known as a Web address.

Vertical scroll bar Allows the user to quickly move up and down in a Web page.

Virtual community A site in cyberspace where people gather to discuss topics of mutual interest, make friends, and form relationships.

Virtual shopping malls Groups of online storefronts where companies market their goods and services on the World Wide Web. *See also* online shopping.

Virtual storefront A Web site established by a company wishing to create a unique and individual business, or commercial, presence on the Web. *See also* Web site.

W3 *See* World Wide Web.

Web *See* World Wide Web.

Web address Unique string of text that identifies the location of a Web page on the World Wide Web. *See also* Uniform Resource Locator.

Web browser Computer program that enables users to find, view, and interact with Web sites on the World Wide Web. Web browsers offer easy-to-use point and click environments to quickly access information on the Web.

Web ethics Guidelines that provide advice on how to behave properly when interacting and publishing on the Web.

Web document *See* Web page.

Web page A specially formatted file designed for use on the World Wide Web that enables the user to display Web pages in a Web browser. Web pages typically include text, graphics, and links to other Web pages, and may also include sound and video clips. Also referred to as Web document. *See also* hyperlink.

Web presentation A collection of Web pages, or documents, that are organized and designed to present a cohesive message and disseminate information.

Web Publishing Wizard A step-by-step way to automate the process of making your Web pages accessible on the Web.

Web server A computer or a network of computers that stores Web pages and makes them available on the Web.

Web site A collection of linked Web pages that has a common theme or focus.

Webmaster The manager of a Web site.

Webring A group of Web pages related to a topic and linked together to form a ring, or circle. Each page in a Webring is connected by a forward and backward link.

Windows Upgrades An Internet Explorer add-on that includes updated versions of applications installed with Windows and new utilities.

World Wide Web (WWW) A vast series of electronic documents called Web pages or Web documents that are linked together over the Internet. *See also* Web page.

WYSIWYG What-you-see-is-what-you-get, a feature that allows the user who is editing to view formatting and enhancements as they would appear on a finished page.

Index

Index

Index